10 Ways to Say "I Love You"

10 Ways to Say "I Love You"

Josh McDowell

HARVEST HOUSE PUBLISHERS
EUGENE, OREGON

Cover by Dugan Design Group, Bloomington, Minnesota

Cover photo © Lev Dolgachov / Alamy

10 COMMITMENTS is a series trademark of The Hawkins Children's LLC. Harvest House Publishers Inc. is the exclusive liscensee of the trademark 10 COMMITMENTS.

10 WAYS TO SAY "I LOVE YOU"
Copyright © 2015 by Josh McDowell Ministry. All rights reserved.
Published by Harvest House Publishers
Eugene, Oregon 97402
www.harvesthousepublishers.com

Library of Congress Cataloging-in-Publication Data
   McDowell, Josh, author.
   10 ways to say "I love you" / Josh McDowell.
      pages cm
   Includes bibliographical references.
   ISBN 978-0-7369-5387-0 (pbk.)
   ISBN 978-0-7369-5388-7 (eBook)
   1. Marriage—Religious aspects—Christianity. I. Title. II. Title: Ten ways to say "I love you".
   BV835.M3375 2015
   248.8'44—dc23

                  2014021855

Printed in the United States of America

    14 15 16 17 18 19 20 21 22 23 / VP-JH / 10 9 8 7 6 5 4 3 2 1

ACKNOWLEDGMENTS

I wish to recognize the following individuals for their valuable contribution to this book.

Dave Bellis, my friend and colleague for over 36 years, for collaborating with me on the outline of this book, pulling from my talks and other works to then write the rough draft, and folding in all the edits and revisions to shape this work into its final form. I recognize Dave's insight on the topics of marriage and relationships, and I'm deeply grateful for his contribution.

Becky Bellis for laboring at the computer to ready the manuscript.

Terry Glaspey of Harvest House for his vision and guidance in shaping the direction and tone of this work.

Paul Gossard of Harvest House for his expert editing and the insight he brought to the manuscript completion.

Last but not least is *Dottie, my wife,* for her written contribution in this book, for her love and patience toward me, and for her over 40 years in a devoted journey with me that has unlocked the secrets of loving.

Contents

1

What Do You
Want in a Relationship?

Working late one night, I jumped when my concentration was broken by a phone call.

"Mr. McDowell?"

The young woman on the line hardly waited for me to respond.

"I've been married six months," she said, "and already the honeymoon is over. Tonight my husband went out with the guys after we had a big argument. I feel alone and rejected. I sat here thinking, *Is this all there is to it?*" Obviously depressed, her voice cracking with emotion, she concluded, "Please tell me there is something more."

This woman had some idea of what she expected in a relationship, and what she was experiencing wasn't it. She repeated her request. "Please tell me there is something more."

"There is," I replied. "It's called an intimate relationship."

Have you longed for a romantic evening with your husband, only to get a few grunts as he watches a basketball or football game? Have you dated and wondered how a fun time with a person could blossom into a committed love? Or have you just wondered how to make a good marriage into a great one?

If you want to know how to spark or enrich a love relationship, you're not alone. The search for a true intimate love is the theme of most hit songs and runs as an undercurrent through most movies. The theme of the secret of loving is the lifeblood of millions of bestselling novels and nonfiction books. And many TV programs reflect and rekindle our dream of a true love that will last. But for many a lasting love relationship remains elusive.

What We Fear

I believe there are two fears that keep many people from experiencing the intimacy and joy of the love relationship they really desire.

One is the fear of never being loved.

The other is the fear of never being able to love.

Let me reassure you that these fears are not abnormal. Many people are like me. I didn't see a true intimate love relationship modeled when I was growing up. My father was the town drunk. He was abusive to my mother, stayed drunk most of the time, and more or less ignored me. I never remember hearing my dad say, "I love you." When I left home I feared that my dysfunctional childhood would carry over into future relationships. I was scared that my emotional baggage would keep me from truly loving and being loved.

The truth is, no one has experienced a perfect home life growing up. There is no such thing as perfect parents who model a perfect love life. So we all have experienced some form of relational dysfunction in our lives—it's just a matter of how dysfunctional we've become. We all have emotional baggage to deal with in life. The big question is how we are going to work through our dysfunction to form a healthy, intimate love relationship with another person that will last.

We live in a culture where love relationships are often short-lived. Many couples live with each other on a "trial basis" because they fear that the marriage won't last if they don't "test" it out first. Recent studies show that "marriages are at an all-time low, and if divorce rates continue to increase the way they have for the past 20 years, then only a minority of couples can expect to be together for over 15 years."[1] Yet at the same time most married and dating couples I know want their relationship to last a lifetime.

So if you want a truly intimate relationship that will last, what do you do?

Quite often I've had a man tell me his relationship with his wife would really be great if she'd get on the same page with him sexually. Many men see sex as the bonding agent in their marriage and the key ingredient to make it last. It's like love and sex are synonymous in their minds. They think if you love someone you're going to have great sex, and if you have great sex it must mean you're really in love. Reality is, that is simply not the case.

Sex is a major factor in developing an intimate love relationship between a man and a woman—there is no doubt about that. And this is confirmed on a biological level. Researchers have discovered a hormone called *oxytocin*, nicknamed the "cuddle hormone." Oxytocin is a chemical your brain releases during sex and the activity leading up to it. When this chemical is released, it prompts feelings of caring, trust, and deep affection. The purpose is to create a deep bond or attachment to the other person.

Every time you have sex, your body has a chemical reaction—the release of oxytocin—that tells you to be intimate with that person. That is one of the primary purposes of sex—to lead to an intimate relationship. But that's only part of the dynamic. Relational intimacy isn't achieved by simply engaging in a physical sex act. Human sexuality involves every aspect of a person's being—physical, emotional, spiritual, and relational. And sex is meant to connect us on every level.

Over the years I have encountered scores of married couples wanting to know why they have lost the intimacy in their relationship. They have sex physically, but they are missing that deep love connection on every level. It's as if sex as a physical pleasure is separate from their emotional and relational lives. It is something they do rather than being a way of expressing the deep love they have for each other. Truth is, a fantastic sex life isn't the cause of a great relationship. Rather, an intimate, close relationship on every level results in a fantastic sex life.

The point is, *nothing good is going to happen in bed between a husband and wife unless good things have been happening between them before they go to bed.* Sex is an important factor in a relationship, but sexual involvement is no cure for an anemic relationship. Many people are willing to give time, energy, and money to become better sex partners, but neglect the nurture of the essential skills of caring, loving, and becoming relationally intimate.

Would you like to experience a deep emotional connection and bonding of your inner spirit with another person until you know beyond all doubt you have found your true soul mate? Perhaps you know the one you love is the one for you and you're married to him or her. Would you like to take that relationship to a whole new level of intimacy? That is what we are here to discover. On our journey together we want to show you how to develop a true and intimate love relationship with each other.

Love, true love, isn't something you fall into. Cupid's arrow doesn't just strike you and *boom*, you're in love. Soul mates don't magically appear overnight. True intimacy is developed, formed, and shaped into a lifelong love relationship. A love relationship deepens and grows when two people understand what love is and then take the committed steps necessary to nurture that love. It's not simply about emotional feelings, it's about a commitment to love someone for life. Feelings come and go but loving someone is about choosing—specific love choices that happen day in, day out.

Commit to Making Ten Love Choices

It was a long time ago, but I vividly remember the words of the minister when he asked me, "Will you, Joslin David, take Dorothy Ann to be your wedded wife? To have and to hold from this day forward, for better or worse, for richer, for poorer, in sickness and in health, to love and to cherish 'til death do you part?"

The end of that ceremony wasn't the conclusion of my marriage to Dottie. It was the beginning. A love relationship, especially a marriage, isn't a destination, it is a relational journey on which the travelers are bonded together by a lifetime of love choices. On that wedding day I made a solemn vow, a commitment, to choose to love Dottie every day for the rest of my life. She committed to the same. And the choices we have made have blossomed into a relationship that has provided us all the meaning, happiness, and joy we could ever hope to experience.

Dottie and I have actually made ten commitments reflected in ten very specific love choices that have produced and continue to produce a deep, intimate love relationship between us. I contend that if you commit to these love choices you will discover the true secret of loving too.

Your commitment to make certain love choices will be flawed. Understand that up front. You are human and humans are flawed. While you won't be able to deliver on every commitment perfectly, you can choose to love to the best of your ability. The following love choices can be your heartfelt attempts, your honest endeavors, your earnest striving to fulfill these commitments and keep making them. Love—intimate love—is a journey of loving and being loved. With that in mind I challenge you to make these ten commitments—ten ways you choose to love your spouse by

1. making God a priority in my life
2. loving and accepting myself
3. being a fantastic lover
4. becoming a great listener
5. learning the art of communication
6. demonstrating an accepting, loyal, enduring love
7. resolving conflicts quickly
8. always forgiving

9. making money matter

10. keeping my love life fresh and alive

Did you notice that none of these love choices is dependent upon the performance of your spouse or another person? It's true that relationship is a two-way street, and you of course want the person you love to reciprocate by making these choices too. But this book is for you and these are choices *you alone* can commit to make regardless of what anyone else does. By making these choices you will more clearly understand what love really is and what is required to truly love another. These are love choices that will lead you down a path of becoming an absolutely irresistible lover. You will be building and nurturing yourself so you can be the kind of person who is caring and considerate, patient and not easily offended, giving and not demanding of your own way, understanding and forgiving. Does that sound like an attractive lover to you? I suspect every man, husband, woman, or wife would want that kind of person as their lifelong partner and lover.

In other words, committing to these love choices is first and foremost about developing yourself into a great lover and lifelong partner in marriage. The golden rule of a happy and fulfilling marriage might be stated like this: "Whatever qualities you desire in your spouse, develop first in yourself."

I posed a question when I phrased the title of this first chapter: "What do you want in a relationship?" If you were to answer that question you might think about what qualities you want in a spouse or what you really want out of a love relationship. However, by committing to make these ten love choices you are not so much focusing on what you hope to get out of a love relationship but rather what you are willing to put into it. Committing to these choices isn't so much about what you get, but what you are able to give. It isn't about changing someone else, it's about you becoming a changed lover. This book is designed to empower you with choices that transform you into a person who is free to give without having to get in return. It is about you becoming a person who knows what love truly is and what it takes to develop a deep intimate love relationship—a relationship that can grow more meaningful every day and can last a lifetime.

In the pages that follow we will learn how you can commit to make these love choices an everyday reality in your life. I encourage you to share this book with your spouse or the person you are seriously involved with. Tell him or her you are taking steps to become a better lover, which will lead to a deepened intimate relationship with him or her. In effect you are saying, "Join me in a journey to discover how we can grow deeper in love with each other." Reading this book together and comparing notes can be fun and enriching.

So let's get started. And the place to start is with God—the One who is the embodiment of love. He is the one who created humans to love. How we relate to him has a great deal to do with how we relate to others. That's the topic of the next chapter.

2

I Choose to Love You by
Making God a Priority in My Life

The phone rang. The person on the other end sounded depressed. "Josh, I need your help," Brad stated bluntly. Coming to the point quickly he added, "Emily and I are drifting apart and I'm not motivated to do much about it."

I agreed to meet with Brad for breakfast. Emily and Brad had been married eight years. Both attended church regularly and were thought of as mature Christians. They both were strong leaders in our small community. Brad wasted no time cutting to the chase when we met.

"Josh," Brad began, "you've spoken a lot about love and relationships and I need some real guidance. I hope you can help me."

"Well, I hope I can help too," I said. "What's going on?"

"Well," Brad continued, "Emily and I had a little argument last night and I said something that really hurt her. After things had cooled down a bit, we were getting ready for bed when she just put it out there, 'Brad, do you love me anymore?'" Brad took a sip of his coffee before continuing.

"And, Josh, I waited for the longest time to answer and then finally just said, 'I don't know, Em. I just don't know anymore.' And Josh, I know it's not right but things have just grown cold between us. I'm afraid both of us seem to have lost the motivation to get our marriage back on track."

What was developing between Brad and Emily was emotional distance. Their relationship was growing cold and their marriage was becoming stale. What Brad was looking for was something to spark his motivation to salvage a marriage that was going south. As I probed Brad, I learned that nothing major had happened recently between him and Emily to make it worse. The two of them simply seemed to have drifted apart.

I put down my cup of coffee and leaned toward Brad and spoke softly. "How's your spiritual life, Brad?" I asked. "Do you feel close to God? Are you praying regularly for Emily? Do you long to please God like you used to?"

The expression on Brad's face told me he was puzzled by my questions. With a little irritation in his voice he said, "I've got a relational problem with Emily, not a spiritual problem with God. Yes, I'm okay with him—it's Emily I'm struggling with."

Marriage: A Three-Way Proposition

What I wanted to lead Brad to understand is that his relationship with God and his relationship with Emily were intrinsically tied together. I wanted him to see that God could become the main spark—the needed motivator—to revitalize his relationship with Emily.

Many couples have bought into a common misconception about marriage. They think that an intimate love relationship in marriage is primarily the result of just the horizontal relationship between a husband and wife. They feel that each one has the responsibility to love the other, remain committed, and when needed energize their motivation to keep their love life alive and well. If marriage were solely designed to be between two people on a horizontal level, they of course would be correct. But marriage isn't just a horizontal relationship—it also includes a vertical relationship.

Marriage is a relationship between a man, a woman, and God. From the very beginning God intended marriage to be a three-way proposition. He is clearly involved in the marriage relationship. He created a male in his image. He created a female in his image. And then he invited them to join him in his perfect circle of relationship—the triune Godhead of Father, Son, and Holy Spirit. God's purpose all along was for humans to enjoy an intimate relationship with him. He didn't create the first couple and say, "Okay I've created you two as relational beings so go off in the garden and relate—I'm out of here!" No, he wanted to be a partner in this relationship called marriage.

Jesus was asked if a man could divorce his wife for any reason.

> "Haven't you read the Scriptures?" Jesus replied. "They record that from the beginning 'God made them male and female.' And he said, 'This explains why a man leaves his father and mother and is joined to his wife, and the two are united into one. Since they are no longer two but one, let no one separate them, for God has joined them together'" (Matthew 19:4-6 NLT).

God is the binding agent within a marriage. With his power and love, he is present so that the two people joined as one may discover and delight in what he is all about—relationships. He created marriage, and he will be an active partner with a married couple if they will allow him. He is there in your marriage! And he feels the pain of any couple like Brad and Emily, whose love for each other grows cold.

This may sound strange to you, but when you neglect your spouse and emotionally hurt the one you love, you also cause pain to another love of your life—Jesus. He loves your spouse as much as he loves you, and he feels his or her pain because he is part of your marriage relationship.

Jesus tells us there will come a time when he will invite his redeemed children into the kingdom of heaven. He will say to them, "I was hungry, and you fed me. I was thirsty, and you gave me a drink. I was a stranger, and you invited me into your home. I was naked, and you gave me clothing. I was sick, and you cared for me. I was in prison, and you visited me" (Matthew 25:35-36).

And his children will ask when they saw him hungry, thirsty, a stranger, naked, sick, or in prison. And Jesus will say "I tell you the truth, when you did it to one of the least of these my brothers and sisters, you were doing it to me!" (Matthew 25:40).

I wanted Brad to realize that when he was there caring for and loving his wife, it was like caring for Jesus. That is a powerful motivator. I wanted Brad to realize that marriage is a three-way proposition. Jesus was there loving Brad's wife with tender care but was doing it alone because Brad had drifted away from her emotionally. And he was failing to meet Emily's deep needs on a human level. It was as if Jesus were to say to Brad, "I was emotionally hungry, and you didn't feed me. I was emotionally thirsty, and you didn't give me anything to drink...I was emotionally vulnerable and naked and you left me alone. I was emotionally sick, and you didn't come to my aid. Because when you began to abandon Emily in her emotional need, it was as if you were abandoning me too." That is powerful motivation to meet the needs of our spouses. It is a thrilling thought that in a way we delight Jesus when we minister to our spouses.

My Misconception About Putting God First

Early in my ministry Dottie traveled with me from city to city. She enthusiastically embraced my speaking ministry, and in many ways she was my partner in ministry. As we began to have children, it became difficult for her to be on the road with me. So she settled down in one place to make the "McDowell home" while I still kept a packed schedule of traveling all over the country.

Dottie was fine with this arrangement because she understood what my speaking ministry was all about. At the same time, raising a family while the husband and dad was out speaking wasn't easy. I remember at one point she shared how difficult it was beginning to be doing things on her own. I had told her to speak up anytime my schedule put too much of a strain on her. And she did.

I have to admit I struggled a little with my loyalties. I wanted to be there for Dottie, while at the same time keep God first in my life. How was I going to keep making him a priority in ministry and still attend to the needs of my family? I thought when push came to shove, he had to come first and my family second.

I'm sure glad I had chosen to make myself accountable to a few wise and more mature men at that time in my life, because they gave me wise counsel. I remember that my accountability partners helped me understand a few passages of Scripture about putting God first in my life.

The apostle Peter directed husbands this way: "You husbands must give honor to your wives. Treat your wife with understanding as you live together...Treat her as you should so your prayers will not be hindered" (1 Peter 3:7). Jesus said, "You must love the Lord your God with all your heart, all your soul, and all your mind [and] love your neighbor as yourself" (Matthew 22:37-39). The apostle John wrote, "Let's not merely say that we love each other; let us show the truth by our actions" (1 John 3:18).

It took me back a little at first to think that if I didn't treat Dottie with honor and understanding, my prayers would be hindered. That was a big deal to me. I also realized that loving God with my everything was directly tied to loving my neighbor, and my wife was my closest neighbor. Finally, my love of Dottie couldn't just be words spoken on a long-distance call; I had to put my love in action. It didn't take long to see that God wanted Dottie and my family to be my primary ministry. Showing love and care to her and the kids then became the platform to minister to others. Putting God first was actually lived out and expressed in loving and attending to my closest neighbor, my wife.

That perspective changed everything. I didn't stop traveling, but my speaking schedule took on a whole new dimension. My schedule began to revolve around loving and caring for my wife and children first. Living with the woman I loved in an understanding way kept my prayers to God from being hindered. Together he, Dottie, and I began to make a great marriage! We still enjoy a great marriage. That isn't to say I still don't struggle with demonstrating my commitment to Dottie while maintaining a busy schedule—I do. But it makes all the difference in the world when I see that God wants me to love him with my everything and love my closest neighbor (Dottie) as myself.

What Does God Want out of Your Marriage?

If you accept God as part of your marriage, then what is it that he wants out of the relationship? Does he want you to obey him and follow the commands of Scripture, go to church, give tithes and offerings, raise your kids to be Christians, and so on? What do you think he really wants from you and your spouse?

It's true that God wants all of us to obey Scripture. But there is something more basic than that. He does want obedience, but for a very good reason. He gets something out of you loving him and you loving your spouse.

Jesus taught his followers all the laws of Moses. He wanted them to be devoted to him and the commands of Scripture. Yet he shared the bottom line of *why* he really wanted their devotion—something that goes for each of us too. He said, "I have told you this so my joy may be in you and that your joy may be complete" (John 15:11 NIV). That is what God wants out of your marriage. He wants your relationship to be filled with his joy. It makes him happy when you are loving your spouse. When you live with your wife in an understanding way it makes him happy and it gives you joy. When you brag on your husband and lift him up to others for being faithful and true, it gives God joy and it makes you happy too. Following his commands—to love unselfishly, be kind and gracious, patient and caring—gives him joy and brings joy and fulfillment to your marriage relationship too.

Scripture is full of commands to follow, and God put them there for your good. He knows if you follow in his path you will have a life full of joy, and that makes him incredibly happy.

King David and his own son, King Solomon, wrote,

> Joyful are people of integrity,
>> who follow the instructions of the LORD.
> Joyful are those who obey his laws
>> and search for him with all their hearts
>>> (Psalm 119:1-2).

> Make me walk along the path of your commands,
>> for that is where my happiness is found
>>> (Psalm 119:35).

> This is my happy way of life:
>> obeying your commandments
>>> (Psalm 119:56 NLT).

> My child, listen to what I say,
>> and treasure my commands.
> Tune your ears to wisdom,
>> and concentrate on understanding…
> Then you will understand what is right, just and fair,
>> and you will find the right way to go.
> For wisdom will enter your heart,
>> and knowledge will fill you with joy.
> Wise choices will watch over you.
>> Understanding will keep you safe
>>> (Proverbs 2:1-2,9-11).

When we love God with everything we are and love our spouse—our closest neighbor—as we love ourselves, we experience joy and that gives him pleasure. He is in our relationship to guide us and direct us in his ways so we can maximize our relationship with our spouse and with one another. Making him a priority in our lives and marriage pays great dividends.

The Best Handbook on Love, Sex, and Marriage

While lecturing on the Christian perspective on love, sex, and marriage in a psychology class at a Northeastern university, I was asked by a student, "What are some factors that produce a good marriage?" After listing both the negative and positive factors, I asked the class where they thought I had come up with the list. Most replied they thought they came from a book on marriage, or a psychology or sociology textbook. You should have seen their response when I pointed out that these are positive and negative factors of an intimate relationship as depicted in the Bible.

The best handbook on love, sex, and marriage is given to us from a God who wants each of us to have maximum joy in marriage, which greatly pleases him. Here are the positive factors from Scripture that produce a good marriage, contrasted with the negative.

POSITIVE	NEGATIVE
Patient: James 1:2-4; Hebrews 10:16; 1 Corinthians 13:4; Colossians 3:12-13	Impatient
Seeking the good of others: 1 Corinthians 13:5; Philippians 2:4; Galatians 6:2	Seeking one's own good
Giving: Luke 6:38; 1 John 4:10	Taking
Selfless: Philippians 2:3-8	Selfish
Truthful: Colossians 3:9; Zechariah 8:16; 1 Corinthians 13:6; Ephesians 4:25	Lying

Humble: Philippians 2:3-8; Proverbs 16:18; James 4:6; Colossians 3:12	Proud
Kind: 1 Corinthians 13:3; Matthew 5:21,22; Colossians 3:12; Galatians 5:22	Hating and con-trolled by hate
Trusting: Proverbs 27:4; 1 Corinthians 13:4,7	Distrustful; jealous
Realistic view of self: 1 Corinthians 4:6-7; 8:1; 13:4; Colossians 2:18; Galatians 6:4	Arrogant; conceited
Responsible: Luke 16:10-12	Irresponsible
Protective of others: 1 Corinthians 13:5-6	Thinks of own reputation
Forgiving: Colossians 3:13; Matthew 11:25; 6:14	Unforgiving
Self-examining: Matthew 7:1-2; John 8:9; Luke 6:37	Judgmental
Content: Jude 15:18; Hebrews 13:5	Complaining
Gratitude: Proverbs 19:3; 1 Thessalonians 5:8; Romans 1:21; Ephesians 5:20	Ingratitude
Self-controlled/even-tempered: Proverbs 16:32; Romans 5:3-4; 1 Corinthians 13:5; Galatians 5:23	Self-indulgent/temper uncontrolled
Diligent: James 4:17; Colossians 3:23	Complacent

Keeps confidentialities: 1 Corinthians 13:7; 1 Peter 2:9; 1 Timothy 5:13	Gossips
Gentle: Galatians 5:23; Colossians 3:12	Harsh
Compassionate: Colossians 3:12; Luke 6:28; Galatians 6:2	Uncompassionate
Sensitive/courteous/polite: 1 Corinthians 13:5	Rude
Faithful: Galatians 5:22	Unfaithful

God's Word is the best handbook on marriage, and the Holy Spirit can guide you in applying its positive truths to your relationship. God wants your marriage to be rich and fulfilling. And as you and your spouse continue to make him a priority in your lives, he will teach you to become fantastic lovers.

Let me ask you the question I asked Brad at the beginning of this chapter. How is your spiritual life? Do you feel close to God? Are you praying regularly for your spouse or loved one?

You may go to church occasionally and think of yourself as a Christian, but question the depth of your relationship with God. If he feels distant, then you need to know him for who he really is, the "God who is passionate about his relationship with you" (Exodus 34:14 NLT).

The following is a simple presentation of how to truly experience a relationship with God. If you take the step to place your trust in Christ or recommit your life to him, share your commitment with a friend. And then get connected with other followers of Christ in a small group and church. Pursue your relational journey with Christ and realize he wants to be a vital part of your love life and marriage.

How to Experience a Relationship with God

Placing your trust in Christ as your Savior involves four things.

1. Understand that God loves you and wants a relationship with you.

    - You have been created in his image.
    - You are special to him.
    - He longs for his relationship with you to complete you and empower you to have loving relationships with others, especially your spouse.

2. Recognize there is a problem.

    - "All have sinned; all fall short of God's glorious standard" (Romans 3:23).
    - "When people sin, they earn what sin pays—death" (Romans 6:23 NCV).
    - "Those who do not know God...will be punished with everlasting destruction and shut out from the presence of the Lord" (2 Thessalonians 1:8-9 NIV).

3. Realize your sin has brought death and separated you from God. So you are helpless to gain life and favor with him, but...

    - "God showed his great love for us by sending Christ to die for us while we were still sinners" (Romans 5:8).
    - "God made Christ, who never sinned, to be the offering for our sin, so that we could be made right with God through Christ" (2 Corinthians 5:21).
    - "There is salvation in no one else! There is no other name

[Jesus] in all of heaven for people to call on to save them"
(Acts 4:12).

This means that despite your helpless state, you can enter into new
life—a new life in Christ. Yet this is not through your own efforts;
it is by the work of Jesus and his sacrificial death for you. This new
life includes…

- having your life and joy made complete through a relationship with Christ.

- discovering your purpose and meaning in life.

- experiencing deepened and fulfilling love relationships
  with others.

- embracing your sense of belonging in community with
  other followers of Christ and realizing your true mission
  in life.

4. In order to accept this new relationship with Christ you
   must…

   - believe that Jesus is who he said he was—the Son of
     God (John 8:24).

   - turn your back on your old life—repent of your sin
     (Ephesians 4:22).

   - cry out to God for mercy as King David did in the Old
     Testament when he prayed, "Listen to my pleading, O
     LORD. Be merciful and answer me! My heart has heard
     you say, 'Come and talk to me' [have a relationship with
     me]. And my heart responds, 'LORD, I am coming'"
     (Psalm 27:7-8).

   - Place your trust in Jesus as the one who will give you a
     new life and make you right before God.

If you are prepared to commit—or recommit—to a relationship with God, pray…

- God, I *embrace* the reality that you love me and desire an eternal relationship with me.

- I *recognize* that I am a sinner and I can do nothing to gain your favor or forgiveness.

- I *realize* that Jesus is my only hope. Based on your sacrificial death for me, I ask you to forgive me of all my sins. Right now I turn my back on my old life.

- I *respond* to you right now, Jesus, by placing my trust in you as my Savior. In faith I believe you will make me right before God, transforming me into his child and giving me an eternal relationship with you.

I *thank you* for your grace—your mercy to me. Thank you for forgiving me and making me right before God. Thank you for showing me your heart of love and bringing me into a relationship with you. I pray all this in the name of Jesus. Amen.

Commitment #2

I Choose to Love You by Loving and Accepting Myself for Who I Am

Ron's hugs felt tender yet strong to Michelle. Whenever he would wrap his arms around her she felt safe and secure. But somehow she didn't feel his love in the way she wanted. It was as if she couldn't quite touch his inner being. And she didn't sense he was deeply connecting with her. Michelle sensed there was something that kept Ron from feeling her love toward him, but she didn't know what the problem was.

Ron was a handsome, well-groomed executive type. He conveyed an air of confidence that exemplified the principles he taught as a financial planner. His confident handshake and positive demeanor communicated success and assertiveness. So why was he coming to me about his marriage?

I had just finished speaking on the importance of having a healthy self-image. Ron pulled me aside and said, "Josh, I really need what you're talking about because I'm running scared most of the time." I asked him to sit down and explain.

"I know I come off as self-assured," he began. "But deep inside I'm afraid people will see me for who I really am—a mess and a failure. I've been married less than a year and I'm scared to death my wife isn't going to keep loving me once she sees me for the real me."

In my conversation with Ron I learned he grew up in a verbally abusive home. He repeatedly heard his father say things like "Don't be so stupid, Ron," "What's wrong with you—can't you do anything right?" and "You're not going to amount to anything—you're just worthless."

As an adult Ron proved his dad wrong. He was "successful" in his career, but down deep he saw his relational life as "a mess and a failure." Ron's poor self-image was keeping his affectionate wife at an emotional arm's length. When he looked at himself he didn't like what he saw, so he found it difficult to love and accept himself for who he was, and it was negatively affecting his marriage. Reality is, sometimes we fail at relationships simply because we don't have a good relationship with ourselves.

How Do You See Yourself?

They say the camera doesn't lie. But I disagree and I think I can prove it. Pull out your driver's license and take a look at it. Are you proud of the "mug shot" staring back at you? Do you like what you see? I hate mine—it looks terrible. The people at the DMV have no skills whatsoever at taking portraits. The "personal identification photos," as they call them, don't come close to looking like who we are, do they?

Well, each of us carries another personal identification photo, one that is far more important than the one we carry in a wallet or purse. It is an emotional or inner self-portrait we have of ourselves. When you look at the inner you, do you like what you see? Or are you like Ron, finding it difficult to love and accept yourself for who you are?

Your ability to love and accept yourself for who you are directly affects your ability to love your spouse and others around you. Some people may claim it's selfish to love yourself, but the truth is that loving yourself is a prerequisite to loving others. And that truth comes from a very authoritative source—the Bible and Jesus himself.

The Importance of Loving Yourself Unselfishly

Jesus said that you are to love God with all you are and then "love your neighbor as yourself" (Matthew 22:39). Jesus is certainly indicating we are to love ourselves, but he isn't advocating a narcissism that focuses on a selfish pursuit in life. Rather he is acknowledging your intrinsic value and worth as God's creation and that it is proper to provide for and protect what he has made.

Say it's one of those days when everything seems to go wrong. You head home from work tired and hungry. As you walk through the door the smell of your favorite meal greets you. Your spouse has gotten off work early and decided to fix you a great meal. Are you being selfish for enjoying a delicious meal and satisfying your hunger? Or perhaps he or she has picked up a couple of DVDs on the way home and suggests an undistracted evening of watching an entertaining movie. Are you being selfish for wanting to relax after a long day?

You feed yourself and find ways to relax, get enough sleep, and protect your body. Is that being selfish? Or are you simply loving yourself in order to take proper care of the physical body God has given you?

The Bible goes on to explain that "husbands ought to love their wives as they love their own bodies. For a man who loves his wife shows love for himself. No one hates his own body but feeds and cares for it, just as Christ cares for the church" (Ephesians 5:28-29). What this passage assumes is that we care enough about ourselves to properly provide for what we need and protect ourselves from harm. It is appropriate and healthy to look out for our own security, happiness, and welfare. We are not being selfish when we do this, we are simply respecting and valuing ourselves as persons created in the image of God with infinite dignity and worth.

When Jesus said, "Do to others whatever you would like them to do to you" (Matthew 7:12), he is working from this same premise: we are to properly love ourselves. If we don't value and love ourselves properly, we are going to have a tough time knowing how to love others as we should.

While I agree that we can become self-centered and all wrapped up in our own self-interests, I don't agree that self-worth and self-love are sinful ideas. In fact, I believe that a proper understanding of our worth and value as God's creation is exactly what keeps us from becoming selfish. The apostle Paul encouraged "everyone among you not to think more highly of himself than he ought to think; but to think so as to have sound judgment, as God has allotted to each a measure of faith" (Romans 12:3 NASB).

Paul is not saying in this verse that we should not think highly of ourselves. He says that we should not think more highly of ourselves than *what we really are*. In other words, we should be realistic in our opinions of ourselves. That's why Paul added that we are "to think so as to have sound judgment." His point is that we should form this opinion or self-portrait as a result of a realistic appraisal of ourselves based on God's view of us. It is not being selfish to accept his view of ourselves; it is being biblical. So a healthy sense of value and worth of ourselves is seeing ourselves as he sees us—no more and no less.

Why You Are Worth Being Loved

Most of us struggle to love and accept ourselves even when we "know" God loves and accepts us. We may seem like a picture of health on the outside but have an unhealthy view of our inner selves. In order to love your spouse or that special person in your life as you love yourself, you need to know and accept why God loves and accepts you.

As a being created by God you are worthy of love for at least three reasons:

1. *God created you lovable.* If you grew up feeling ignored, unwanted, or even despised, the people who conveyed that self-image to you were dead wrong. God makes no

mistakes. You are lovable because he created you in his image—a lovable, relational image.

Before there was a world, before there was time and space, there was relationship. God as three persons in one—Father, Son, and Holy Spirit—has eternally existed as relationship: a loving relationship. The Father has always loved the Son, the Son has eternally loved the Father, and the Holy Spirit has forever loved the Father and the Son. Your lovability has been placed in your relational DNA by God himself. When you accept the reality that you are lovable, you are seeing yourself as he sees you.

2. *God created you valuable.* Anyone who says to you that you are not worth much or are unimportant is deluded. Remember, you are valuable because you were created by God in his very image. He is eternally valuable, and he has made you valuable too.

Even though humans turned their backs on God from the very beginning, that didn't lessen their value in his eyes. He, being without sin, couldn't overlook sin, so he had to separate himself from the first couple. But the human race was too valuable to him to leave them separated from him.

You see, the value of an item is determined by what someone is willing to sacrifice or exchange for it. What was your worth to God? It was the sacrificial death of his only Son. He sent his Son in the form of a human to purchase you back. He considers you worth dying for so he can have a relationship with you. Since you are that valuable to him, you need to agree with him and consider yourself truly valuable in his eyes.

3. *God created you competent.* Perhaps you were always

the last person to complete an important task or to
be chosen for a team sport. As a result, you may view
yourself as incompetent or lacking great potential. But
God doesn't see you that way. If you are his child he
has given you special talents and gifts. He has placed
his Holy Spirit within you to empower you for service.
You are far from incompetent or lacking giftedness.
Since God has entrusted you with special gifts and
empowered you with his Spirit, you can count on it:
you are competent. You can see yourself as competent
because that is how he sees you.

The more clearly you see yourself as lovable, valuable, and competent, the better equipped you are to unselfishly love and accept
yourself for who you are. This is not a matter of just positive thinking. I am not suggesting that you "visualize" these three vital traits
until they are true of you. You are *already* lovable, valuable, and
capable. That's how God made you. Transforming your sense of
worth is a matter of accepting and acting on what is already true.

Because you are lovable you can embrace your sense of belonging.
We all need to sense we belong to someone. We feel we belong when
others are willingly there for us in the good times and bad times.
Belonging is what we sense when we know someone loves us without condition just as we are.

The world is full of people who have suffered greatly from a
lack of unconditional love and acceptance. Just about everyone has
sensed a lack of belonging at some level. The love we received from
others is often imperfect because the people loving us are imperfect. At the very least, we have all experienced a conditional love
that communicated, "I love you because..." or "I will love you if..."
Such a message puts belonging on a performance basis. The ongoing threat is that if we do not perform up to certain standards, we

will not be loved. Conditional love and acceptance leaves our basic hunger to belong unsatisfied.

When you accept yourself as lovable and willingly allow someone to love you for who you are, you are empowered with a sense of belonging. And when you return that love, your spouse or special loved one feels they belong as well.

Because you are valuable you can realize your sense of worth. James has reached the pinnacle of success in his profession. He has written many books, and he lectures about his field of expertise around the world. He drives an expensive sports car, owns a large suburban home, and gives generously to his church and other charities. His peers view him as extremely successful and self-assured.

But when you get to know James well, you learn that he is fearful and insecure. It is this insecurity that has driven him to his positions of success. But it may also drive him to despair because his wife has threatened divorce if he does not do something about his workaholic tendencies.

James, among other things, suffers from a case of unhealthy self-worth. He considers himself to be of little value apart from his business achievement. When he was a child, his home life was unpredictable and often painful. His alcoholic father would beat him for no apparent reason. Once he sold his son's bicycle and used the money for liquor. James never knew what his father would do next. As a teenager, he determined to insulate himself from such insecurity by becoming as successful and wealthy as he could.

People like James are all around us today. They see themselves as having little intrinsic value because, in effect, someone communicated they were of little worth. This message comes through clearly when the basic need for security goes unmet. Children who grow up feeling unsafe because of a parent's abuse or emotional neglect feel they are not worth caring for. Like James, these children come into adulthood with an inner portrait that is captioned "unworthy."

When you accept the reality that you are valued by your Creator God, you realize you are worthy of love. You are worth loving: when that realization connects to your emotions, you are empowered to give others the sense that they too are worth loving.

Because you are competent you can gain your sense of confidence. God created everyone with certain abilities and competencies. Every human being is able to say, "I am capable of making worthwhile contributions to others. I can do something." In an ideal environment, children grow up with a healthy sense of competence. The encouragement, support, and appreciation of loving parents spark them to try new things and to overcome difficulties. With a solid base of encouragement and support, children learn to persevere, succeeding in some areas and striving to improve in others.

Your parents played an important role in developing your sense of competence. Think about when you were learning to walk. With the help of your parents, you took your first halting steps, then fell. Hearing your parents' approval and encouragement, you tried again, eventually taking many successive steps before falling again. Your parents probably smiled and applauded and said, "Good try! You can do it!" Before long you were walking everywhere. Even though you don't remember learning to walk you gained the confidence and ability to do it.

But what would you think of a parent who discouraged a child from walking? Baby pulls himself up on unsteady legs, and Dad pushes him down again, saying something like, "You'll never learn to walk, so don't even try." Who could be so cruel as to block a child's attempt to walk? It is unthinkable. Yet many of us have grown up with a similar kind of negative input to our emotions.

Chris was not athletically gifted, but he loved baseball. When he turned nine, he bugged his dad until he agreed to take him to Little League tryouts at the local park. He was so excited at the prospect of signing up to play that he was wild with his practice throws. Before the tryout session was over, his dad said, "Come on, Chris, we're going home. You're not any good at baseball."

Chris's frail confidence in his limited ability was shattered. It took him many years to recover a sense that he could do anything well. Self-doubt still plagues him as an adult.

You may or may not have developed skills and talents as a child. If you did you probably have gained a sense of inner confidence. And if that is the case, you can accept the reality that God has gifted you in some way. If you find it difficult to sense your competence, focus on who he has gifted you with—his very Spirit. God has entered your life for a reason. The primary reason is to demonstrate his love to you by making you one with him (see John 17:21-23). He also enters your life to make you competent. "There are different kinds of service, but we serve the same Lord. God works in different ways, but it is the same God who does the work in all of us. A spiritual gift is given to each of us so we can help each other" (Romans 12:5-7). When you accept the reality that you are a competent and capable person, you gain the courage and power to use those gifts for good, especially loving others.

God created you to be lovable, valuable, and competent. If these areas of your life were affirmed during your developmental years, you probably have a healthy sense of worth and you can more easily love and accept yourself for who you are. But if not, simply reading words to accept yourself doesn't do much. Reversing years of negative emotional programming isn't easy, but it is possible. I'm a living example of it.

How to Accept Yourself for Who You Are

As I indicated earlier, I had a rough home life. Feeling I was lovable, valued, and competent was really out of the picture. You would think I would never have had a chance for a love relationship. But by God's grace, I broke the cycle of dysfunction and learned to accept who I was so I could love my wife and neighbors as I loved myself. But it was a long road.

Apart from growing up in a highly dysfunctional alcoholic home, I was made to feel inferior at school. First, my second-grade teacher tried to switch me from being left-handed. This isn't done in the schools today, but back then, I would be taken to a room with a teacher to practice being right-handed, two afternoons per week, while my friends were out playing softball and basketball. She would give me various tasks to do or things to build. Whenever I started to use my left hand she would reach over with a heavy wooden ruler and... *whack!* Of course, I would immediately withdraw my hand.

As a result of that treatment I developed a speech impediment. Whenever I felt tired, nervous, or scared, I would begin to stutter. I can remember having to get up in class and recite the Gettysburg Address. I just stood there in front of my classmates, stammering, and the teacher kept repeating, "Say it! Say it! Say it!" I finally broke down crying and ran out of the room. It was a less-than-memorable start to a lifetime of public speaking.

The real problem was that no one ever told me they were trying to help me. I concluded that being left-handed proved I was inferior or something even worse. In spite of this, I remained determined that people weren't going to change my left-handedness. And they didn't.

My self-image problems didn't end in the second grade. In the little Michigan elementary school my teachers taught grammar, but I didn't learn it—from either them or my parents. My grammar remained extremely poor. The closest I came to learning anything about correct grammar was from my brother Jim. He was two years older than I was—a sharp guy—and I used to dread his coming home from Michigan State, because every time he came home he would begin correcting my grammar.

I grew fearful of even opening my mouth around Jim. I'd say, "I don't want none of that." He would say, "Don't use a double negative." And I would tell him, "I don't know what no double negative is!"

In my first year at university an English professor was taking roll and asked about a classmate of mine. I blurted out, "He doesn't feel good today!" The professor immediately mocked me, "Mr. McDowell. He doesn't feel *well* today?" That was about the last time I spoke up in class. So, you can see why I believe I was a most unlikely candidate to become a public speaker today.

When Dr. Hampton, my college freshman counselor, looked over my records she observed, "Josh, you're a straight 'D' student. But you've got something that a lot of other people don't have."

"What's that?" I asked, "I'll take anything right now."

"You've got determination and drive," she said. "And that can take you further than most people's minds will ever take them. If you're willing to work at it, I'll be willing to work with you."

I seized the opportunity and spent hour upon hour recording tapes so that she could listen to them to correct my speech. And even though I felt a twinge of resentment every time I was corrected—sort of a *Who do you think you are?* feeling—I knew I was being helped. So I stuck with it.

My low sense of self-worth was also regularly reinforced at my home church and at the Christian college I attended. This was unintentional on their part, of course. But what ministers and Christian leaders would do was to challenge young people to give their talents and gifts to God. The idea was to encourage kids to commit their lives and futures to him. Even after I had become a Christian, I didn't believe that challenge applied to me. You see, I didn't think I had any abilities or assets worth giving. Of course I did, but the unhealthy view I had of myself said otherwise.

During the fall semester of my final year as an undergraduate at Wheaton College I heard a message by Dr. Richard Halverson, who became chaplain of the U.S. Senate. He was speaking on the last night of what we called Spiritual Emphasis Week, and the auditorium was packed. When the invitation came, I thought, *Here we go again.* "Bring your talents, your abilities, your gifts and place them on the altar and say, 'God, here I am. Use me.'"

Hundreds of students did respond. As I sat there wondering why I should have to endure this again, I suddenly stood up and burst out the side door into the night air. I ran all the way to the dorm and tried to go to sleep, but I couldn't.

At about four o'clock in the morning I found myself walking down West Union Street in Wheaton, Illinois. I had reached the end of my proverbial rope, and I just cried out, "God, I've had it." I don't know if my words and attitudes were exactly right or not, but I said, "God, I don't think I have any strengths. I don't think I have any abilities. I've got a bad background. My dad is an alcoholic. I've been sexually abused. I stutter. I've got bad grammar. I can't do this and I can't do that. But here they are—all my limitations and all my shortcomings. Here are my weaknesses. I give them to you. If you can take me for who I am—the good and the bad—and do something with me, I'm yours."

Ever since that desperate prayer things have been different—extraordinarily different. Face it, none of us is perfect. We all have faults and failures and nothing in this life will ever change that. But God accepts us for who we are with all the good, bad, and the ugly. He wants us to do the same. We need to agree with him that we were created in his image and that he felt we were worth dying for. He says he accepts us, so we ought to accept ourselves even though we are imperfect.

That doesn't mean we can live a life of lawlessness and disregard God and people and he will be okay with it. I'm talking about people who have placed their faith in Christ and have become children of God, yet still live imperfectly. He doesn't require perfection in order for us to be loved and accepted. Otherwise we would all be in a world of hurt. But he does require something.

King David from the Old Testament discovered what God wanted from people when we really blow it. At first David thought he wanted a lot of self-loathing, self-effort, trying harder, and making all kinds of sacrifices to him. But when God revealed what he really wanted David wrote this:

> You do not desire sacrifice, or I would offer one. You do not want a burnt offering. The sacrifice you desire is a broken spirit. You will not reject a broken and repentant heart, O God (Psalm 51:17).

All of us are messed up to one degree or another and we seem to keep messing up. As I said, that won't change. Sure, you and I can get better at loving and living, but we are always going to fail somewhere and hurt the ones we love. The key is to have a broken spirit and repentant heart when we do. That is what God wants and, really, that is all that your spouse or that special person in your life wants. Those you love want to know you're sorry when you mess up. I know it's humiliating, but confession is good for the soul, and it's necessary.

You can love and accept yourself, even with all your inabilities, limitations, and failures, when you develop a broken spirit and repentant heart. When you are willing to say you're sorry and admit you blew it, you somehow are elevated to a new level of power to accept yourself. It's a God thing. He "blesses those who are humble" (Matthew 5:5). He doesn't "reject a broken and repentant heart" (Psalm 51:17). Rather, he loves you with an energizing love that enables you to love and accept yourself. He gives you the power to think of yourself in the same way he thinks of you—you are a child who is loved and accepted for who you are.

In many respects your ability to love and accept yourself is determined by what you believe the most important person in your life thinks about you. As we've said, God has already stated your acceptance and worth, and if he is the most important person in your life, then you can love and accept yourself for who you are—his child. Jesus said some very significant things about those who have accepted him.

I have loved you even as the Father has loved me…I have told you these things so that you will be filled with my joy…I no longer call you slaves, because a master does not confide in his slaves. Now you are my friends, since I have told you everything the Father told me. You didn't choose me, I chose you (John 15:9,11,15-16).

The apostle Paul goes on to add to this list of you being loved, a friend of Jesus, and chosen by him. Remember the following things that Paul wrote to believers are *already* true of you. You didn't earn these things or attain them because of some status you may have achieved. This is what God's Word says about you:

- He "purchased [your] freedom with the blood of his Son and forgave [your] sins" (Ephesians 1:7).
- You are a child of God (John 1:12).
- You are "blessed with every spiritual blessing" (Ephesians 1:3).
- "He chose [you] in Christ to be holy and without fault in his eyes" (Ephesians 1:4).
- "God decided in advance to adopt [you] into his family" (Ephesians 1:5).
- You "have received an inheritance from God" (Ephesians 1:11).
- He "seated [you] with him in the heavenly realms" (Ephesians 2:6).
- You "are God's masterpiece" (Ephesians 2:10).
- "You belong to Christ" (Ephesians 2:13 NLT).
- "Nothing can ever separate [you] from God's love" (Romans 8:38).

These are just some of the things God thinks and says about you—his child. Since your heavenly Father is the most important person in your life, believe these things, accept them, and own them as your own. Allow what he thinks and says to reinforce the truth that you are really worth loving. You are not whatever your negative emotions may be telling you. You are who God says you are—nothing more, nothing less.

This isn't just a mind-over-emotional-feelings exercise. I don't believe I could ever have convinced my emotions I was worth loving—not with my background. There were a lot of people involved in helping me reverse the emotional dysfunction. But more than anything I believe my spiritual journey of accepting God's view of me had the greatest impact on my life. I came to love and accept myself for who I am. I've opened up about my painful childhood including my sexual abuse. I shared it first with Dottie and then with others.

It wasn't easy telling my wife about how I had been sexually abused as a child. A sense of shame is generally what a victim feels. As I opened up about what happened, Dottie was very comforting. "I am so sorry that happened to you," she said. As tears streamed down her face she said, "Honey, I so hurt for you."

What she said next truly surprised me. Now, Dottie is a very private person, yet she said, "Josh, you've got to share this with others. God can use your tragic experience to bring hope and healing to others." As Dottie and others helped me to realize I was truly loved for being me and wasn't "damaged goods," I was able to share my story with others.

On my own I don't think I could have gotten past the feeling of being a victim. But with the love of God, my family, and expert counsel, I was discovering who I really was in Christ. My abuser, Wayne Bailey, could not destroy my identity in Christ—he took some things away from me, but he couldn't take that. I am a child of God, created in his image, with infinite value, dignity, and worth.

You may not have been abused as a child, yet there is something very healing about bringing past hurts out in the open and allowing loved ones to comfort you. Opening up to your spouse about your weaknesses and faults is, as I said, good for the soul. Make it a natural part of your relationship with the person you love. As you learn to accept and love yourself for who you are, faults and all, you can truly enjoy a deepened intimacy with another.

4

COMMITMENT #3

I Choose to Love You by Being a Fantastic Lover, Part 1

The audience stands, then looks to the back of the church as the organ plays the traditional "Here Comes the Bride." She is breathtakingly gorgeous.

The groom is a tall, dark, and handsome young man. He watches in rapt fascination as his bride glides toward him with elegance and grace. The smile on her face, the gleam in her eye, and the shape and form of her body excite him as he anticipates their ten-day honeymoon on a tropical island.

At the appointed time he reaches out to take her hand as she steps beside him. Her fragrance fills his senses. He feels his heart beat faster, his breath becomes deeper. Soon he lifts her veil, pulls her close, and kisses her as the minister declares, "I now pronounce you husband and wife."

The groom is a physical-fitness trainer, the bride a professional model. The couple is picture-perfect. The honeymoon suite at the Grand Wailea on Maui is just fabulous. And as the couple retreats into the bedroom the uniting of the two as one physically is beyond description. Neither of them has ever experienced such ecstasy and sheer pleasure. They both describe the other as an absolutely fantastic lover!

Fast-forward three years. The picture-perfect couple is now

divorced. The stated reason on the official court documents: incompatibility.

There was no apparent incompatibility during the honeymoon. They were self-described "fantastic lovers." Yet as exciting as the sexual attraction was, it was not a sufficient bond to hold their married life together. Sex never is the bond, and it was never meant to be.

When a love relationship is based on physical attractiveness and sex appeal alone, it will never last. As exciting as sexual attraction can be, it is such a limited part of a couple's relationship that sex in and of itself simply cannot support the marriage. As I said before, having fantastic sex isn't the cause of a great relationship—but a close, intimate relationship can produce a fantastic sex life.

Sex without enduring love is a lot like a sound. It can be loud, get your attention, and maybe even shatter glass with its intensity, but it lacks meaning. If a sound is going to carry some sense of meaning, it must take on the form and flow of words with substance and purpose.

The apostle Paul put it this way: "If I could speak all the languages of earth and angels, but didn't love others, I would only be a noisy gong or a clanging cymbal" (1 Corinthians 13:1). Sex, even great sex, without a deep abiding love is about as valuable as a clanging cymbal.

Sure, sex may cause physical pleasure and send emotional vibrations up your spine, but to have real purpose, sex must have the relational foundation of love. If you want a love that will last, don't choose to love a body for sexual satisfaction—choose to love a person for an intimate relationship.

What's Love Got to Do with It?

In 1984 musical artist Tina Turner released the hit song "What's Love Got to Do with It?" It portrayed two people trying to have a relationship based on the physical. It simply doesn't work for the long haul. But when you truly understand what love is and pursue a true love for a person, not just a body, it can be the most reward-ing experience in life for a lifetime.

A lot of people can tell you what love does and how it behaves, but can't tell you what it is. For example, people know the Bible says that love acts patiently and is kind. It says love isn't "jealous or boastful or proud or rude. It does not demand its own way" (1 Corinthians 13:4-5). That's the way love operates, but what is love exactly? What is the motivating factor of love?

Jesus identified the motivating factor when he said, "Do to oth-ers whatever you would like them to do to you" (Matthew 7:12). The apostle Paul described love this way: "In humility value others above yourselves, not looking to your own interest but each of you to the interests of others" (Philippians 2:4 NIV). In other words, real love is other-focused.

Paul applied this other-focused love to husbands when he directed them "to love their own wives as their own bodies. He who loves his own wife loves himself; for no one ever hated his own flesh, but nourishes and cherishes it, just as Christ also does the church" (Ephesians 5:28-29 NASB).

With these and other verses we can define what real love is. *Real love*, a love that is other-focused, *makes the security, happiness, and welfare of another person as important as your own.*

To help download the meaning of that, let's look at the words *nourish* and *cherish* in Ephesians 5. It will help us understand how we are to make the security, happiness, and welfare of another as important to us as our own.

Just as we are careful to nourish and cherish our own bodies, we are to nourish and cherish others in love.

To *nourish* means to bring to maturity. It means to care for and contribute to the whole person—relationally, physically, spiritually, and socially. Love is a provider. It requires that we provide for the security, happiness, and welfare of others in order to bring them to maturity just as we provide for our own.

To *cherish* means to protect from the elements. Imagine a nest of newborn eaglets high on a mountain crag, exposed to the sky. An angry thunderstorm is rolling in. The mother eagle swoops down to the nest and spreads her wings over the eaglets to protect them from the pounding rain and swirling wind. That's a picture of what it means to cherish.

Ephesians 5:29 tells us that it is natural for us to cherish ourselves, that is, to protect ourselves from anything that may endanger our mental, physical, spiritual, or social well-being. We buckle up and drive safely to prevent physical injury or death on the highway. We monitor our fat and calorie intake to keep our bodies healthy. In other words, we love ourselves enough to protect ourselves from harm. Love is a protector as well as a provider.

So for a husband to love his wife as he loves himself means he does whatever he can to *provide for* (nourish) the security, happiness, and welfare of his wife relationally, physically, spiritually, and socially, just as he would provide for himself. And he is to *protect* (cherish) his wife from anything that might detour her from or hinder her from achieving maturity, just as he would protect himself.

As I stated earlier, this is the same kind of love Jesus describes in Matthew 27. Everyone is to love their neighbor as themselves. So interestingly enough, a wife should be loving her closest neighbor—her husband—with a providing and protecting love as well.

This is an other-focused love, a true love that is giving and trusting, unselfish and sacrificial, secure and safe, loyal and forever. And because its priority is to protect and provide for the loved one, a fantastic lover will not do things that are harmful to the security, happiness, and welfare of the other person.

Imagine that you and your husband have both had a long day at work. But when you get home, your husband had taken off early; as you enter the house you can smell your favorite meal cooking. The table is already set, a few candles are lit with your best china laid out in perfect order. He has arranged for the kids to stay with his parents for the evening, so you have nothing to do except enjoy a fabulous dinner and spend a relaxing evening with him.

The first thing you would probably do is take a hard look at the man fixing dinner to confirm it is in fact your husband. Once a DNA test and retina scan confirm he is the man you married, you would probably begin a line of questioning. You might suspect he has blown some money irresponsibly, wrecked the family car, or made a commitment to his boss to work during your scheduled family vacation. At any rate, you are probably wondering why he's doing this now. After a few of your "innocent" probing questions, you find everything is just fine. So you settle in for an enjoyable meal.

After dinner your husband insists on cleaning up the dishes. He asks you to relax in the living room until he's finished. He says he'll bring you dessert in a few minutes. This is where your instincts kick in and you're pretty sure there has been a hidden agenda all along and that's *sex*. Surely he isn't doing all this just for your own benefit. He's wanting to be paid back in some way, right? I mean how do most men spell love? You're right, it's *sex*.

To your surprise your considerate husband brings in a tasty dessert and continues the conversation—because he is realizing that you spell love *t-a-l-k*. So he asks about your day, sympathizes with what you struggle with at work, laughs with you about some funny things that happened, and overall is caught up in enjoying your talk together. He is clearly sending the signal that all he wants is to be with you, know how you're doing, and just be there for you as a supportive, caring, and understanding husband so he can give you whatever you need at the moment.

How do you respond to a no-strings-attached expression of caring love? Does it touch your heart that the man you love is saying, "I'm here for you" and that he is not asking for anything in return right now? What does it do for you when your husband indicates he is intrigued with you, wants to discover how you're feeling, know your every thought, and explore your dreams? When you sense your husband finds the inner part of you beautiful and attractive, does it not motivate you to open up and give yourself to him? Isn't that a turn-on? Would it surprise him if at that point you took the initiative and invited him to the bedroom? It shouldn't if he understands that emotional intimacy is the forerunner of physical intimacy.

When your spouse truly makes your security, happiness, and welfare as important as his own, it touches you deeply and revs your engine sexually. The mark of a fantastic lover is the underlying motivation—to give to you, to please you, and to satisfy your every need because you are you. Your lover's fascination with the inner you provides substance and depth to any physical and sexual response. When other-focused love sees sex as an expression of a providing and protective love, a fantastic lover is born.

You can choose to be a fantastic lover who makes the security, happiness, and welfare of your lover as important as your own. You can choose to be other-focused and do your best to nourish or provide for your spouse's best interest. You can choose to cherish or protect him or her from danger or harm. But your choices, as well-meaning as they may be, will run headlong into some blockades. You will encounter hindrances in being other-focused. You will find that some of those hindrances are outside forces. But mostly they will come from within.

Hindrances to Being a Fantastic Lover

Let's face it—being other-focused doesn't come naturally. Reality is, being me-focused is what comes naturally. So if we are going to love others as we love ourselves, we are going to have to resist a couple of driving forces in our lives, and one of those is a spirit of self-reliance.

Self-reliance says, "I can do it myself, I can make it on my own, I don't need a lot of help from you." None of us may come out and verbalize it that way, but when things get tough in life we don't tend to open up and seek help; rather we try to solve problems on our own. This is often a macho approach with us men. We tend to feel that needing someone's help makes us weak. This is a misconception.

CEO with an assistant. Some of this macho thinking comes from a misunderstanding by many men about the role of a husband. I've heard men say, "I am the CEO of my home." A man may think he is responsible to solve problems, make the tough decisions, and be the real leader of the home, meaning he must be a self-reliant leader because biblically he must be the "head" or have authority over his wife.

This misinterpretation of Scripture doesn't just encourage husbands to be self-reliant; it demeans the role of the wife and tends to make her feel she is a second-class citizen in the marriage relationship.

I've heard men say, "Look, I've got to be the leader because the Bible says I'm the head of the wife and a wife is to be 'the helper of the husband.'"

First, the notion that a woman as "helper" is somehow not on equal par with men is incorrect. This idea is simply not biblical.

In Genesis it says that God created human beings in his image and likeness, "male and female he created them" (Genesis 1:27). The woman was made in the same image and likeness of God as the man. Men were not given the superior image of God, with God somehow creating women in a lesser image. Men and women equally share his image.

The Bible also says God made woman as man's "helper." Some have thought this helper role means that he created women as servants or assistants to men. However, the Hebrew word translated "helper" is *ezer*. It denotes one who surrounds, protects, or aids. It is this same word that Jacob used of him when he said, "May the God of your father *help* you" (Genesis 49:25). Moses used it when he said, "The God of my ancestors was my *helper*" (Exodus 18:4).

The psalmist David used it repeatedly in passages like "We put our hope in the LORD. He is our *help* and our shield" (Psalm 33:20).

God is primarily portrayed by the Old Testament writers as the *ezer*—the one who surrounds us and sustains us. This by no means is a lowly servant role. Rather, it is a lofty role to bring help to one who needs it.

When God created a female as a godlike equal to help the male, it was a highly esteemed role, not one of inferiority or servitude. He considered the man to be in need of a woman, and that didn't mean he was inferior either. Women are not inferior for being a counterpart or companion to men, and men are not weak for needing women.

Marriage as a hierarchy. Second, the idea that a husband is in authority over his wife and the wife is to be in submission to her husband has been grossly misunderstood. What many people do is try to apply a hierarchical structure to a marriage relationship. The problem is that being a fantastic lover and achieving relational intimacy isn't about things like authority, control, or who has the last say. It is about unity, oneness of heart, and meeting the needs of one another. That is how the Bible describes the marriage relationship.

Let's read Ephesians 5. Paul says, "Submit to one another out of reverence for Christ. For wives, this means submit to your husbands as to the Lord. For a husband is the head of his wife as Christ is the head of the church" (Ephesians 5:21-23). At first blush this does seem that the Bible is setting up a hierarchical structure for marriage. But when we place this verse within its context we see a different picture.

The context of this passage is Paul explaining how God's people are to praise their Lord for his amazing grace (Ephesians 2:8-9); how he has brought us together as one in his body—the church (Ephesians 2 and 3); how we are to put on a "new nature, created to be like God—truly righteous and holy" (Ephesians 4:24); and how we are to "imitate God, therefore, in everything [we] do" (Ephesians 5:1) by living in the power of his Spirit (Ephesians 5:15-20).

Paul is not attempting to give us insights into a hierarchical structure, but rather into our relationships with each other. He is saying we are now to start acting like God, to be one in our relationship, and to imitate him in all our actions. Then he says, "Submit to one another out of reverence for Christ" (Ephesians 5:21). This admonition is for all of us to submit to one another—not just a certain group of people submitting to those in authority. And Paul is implying that submitting to one another is a key to developing a healthy relationship.

Paul then says that wives are to submit to their husbands, "for a husband is the head [authority] of his wife as Christ is the head of the church" (Ephesians 5:23). At first this may not seem very relational. This passage appears to be saying that wives are to submit to the authority figure—their husbands. That doesn't project a picture of a warm and intimate love relationship between the two. For most of us submission isn't viewed as one of our "love languages." And a husband who sets himself up as a self-reliant authority figure probably isn't a great "turn-on" for his wife. So how is this passage to be interpreted in light of relational oneness and imitating God?

Jesus' model of leadership. We get an insight into the relational dimension of authority by understanding how Christ is head of the church. Jesus' idea of being in authority and how to use the position of leadership is very much different from what is commonly thought and taught. Read his take on leadership:

> In this world the kings and great men lord it over their people, yet they are called "friends of the people." But among you it will be different. Those who are the greatest among you should take the lowest rank, and the leader should be like a servant. Who is more important, the one who sits at the table or the one who serves? The one who sits at the table, of course. But not here! For I am among you as one who serves (Luke 22:24-27).

Jesus was espousing a whole new concept of authority and leadership. The common view was that people subject themselves to leaders and those in authority, who in turn do whatever they want to do. But Jesus taught that leaders are to serve. He shared this revolutionary concept of how to lead during the Passover meal just before he gave his life for the church. John records him getting up from the meal and starting to wash the disciples' feet just as a servant would do. When he finished he said, "Do you understand what I was doing? You call me 'Teacher' and 'Lord,' and you are right, because that is what I am. And since I, your Lord and Teacher, have washed your feet, you ought to wash each other's feet. I have given you an example to follow. Do as I have done to you" (John 13:12-15).

Then how does a husband exercise his authority or headship? By living out Jesus' way of leadership—serving the needs of the wife. This concept of headship as described by Jesus is perhaps difficult for many husbands to grasp. It turns the idea of a self-reliant leader on its head, so to speak. How *do* you effectively lead by serving? How *do* you "call the shots" by taking on the "lowest rank"? This approach is confusing if you try to implement it as a hierarchical structure for marriage. But it really makes sense when you see it in light of developing an intimate relationship with your spouse—a relationship in which you make the security, happiness, and welfare of your wife as important as your own.

Paul goes on, "As the Scripture says, 'A man leaves his father and mother and is joined to his wife, and the two are united as one'" (Ephesians 5:31). Paul was quoting Genesis 2:24, which defines one of the primary purposes of marriage—its unity or intimacy. Paul concludes by saying, "This is a great mystery, but it is an illustration of the way Christ and the church are one. So again I say, each man must love his wife as he loves himself, and the wife must respect her husband" (Ephesians 5:32-33).

Jesus wants the husband and wife to experience oneness and intimacy in the way that Christ and his people (the church) experience intimacy. Jesus made a love choice to humbly serve the needs of his church. We as husbands can make that kind of love choice as well. We can choose to turn our backs on being self-reliant; we can choose instead to follow Jesus and humbly serve the needs of our wives, letting them know how important they are in our lives.

That is quite different from being a self-reliant husband exerting authority as CEO of the home and expecting submission from his wife. That kind of husband gets a low rating as a lover. And he certainly won't be experiencing intimate oneness with his wife. However, the husband who is going to achieve intimacy is the one who makes a love choice to be a humble servant-leader looking out to provide for and protect his wife. Paul says further to husbands, "Love your wives, just as Christ loved the church. He gave up his life for her" (Ephesians 5:25). That kind of loving may be a humbling way to be in relationship with your wife, but it pays off in a deepened, intimate relationship. It honors Jesus.

Making the faith choice. Being self-reliant is a hindrance to becoming a fantastic lover. Another big one is self-centeredness. When you and I are selfishly looking out for number one, we aren't making the security, happiness, and welfare of our spouse as important as our own.

We all can describe self-centered actions. They are all about self. What's very interesting though, is where self-centeredness comes from. Underneath self-centeredness is actually a fear that we won't get what we want or need. So what do we do? We take from others selfishly. And this is a huge hindrance to experiencing intimacy and closeness with those we love.

I remember how early on in my marriage my self-centeredness robbed Dottie and me of feeling close to each other. I'm a public speaker. I like to speak. Dottie is a great listener. She likes to hear what's going on in people's lives. So in our early years I carried over my desire to speak publicly into our private marriage.

After a speaking event I'd talk to Dottie about how it went, how many people were at the event, what they had to say to me after the event, and so on. I'd share what I thought went right, what I thought went wrong, and everything in between. After about an hour or so of my excessive talking I'd ask Dottie how her day went. "Oh, okay I guess." And that would be about it. An unhealthy pattern was emerging: I was the talker, Dottie was the listener. I became the taker, Dottie the giver.

My mentor and dear friend, Dick Day, helped me to see something very important. If I was to achieve the level of intimacy I really desired with Dottie (to be that fantastic lover) I had to make a choice. You might think that choice was to quit talking so much and allow her to talk more. It wasn't that simple.

Back then I had a high need for attention. I still do. Dottie was meeting my need for attention by listening so attentively to me. She was so good at it! She still is. The solution to my self-centeredness wasn't to deny myself attention. That was a valid need in my life. The solution was to address my fear of not getting enough attention by exercising faith in that area. That may sound strange, but I needed to exercise faith in God as my ultimate Provider.

God "gives life and breath to everything and he satisfies every need" (Acts 17:25). Jesus said, "Give, and you will receive…The amount you give will determine the amount you get back" (Luke 6:38). Fear of not getting attention was driving my self-centeredness. If that fear was going to be alleviated, I had to believe that God was willing and able to meet my need. And the way he wanted to meet my need was for me to be a giver, not a taker. I wasn't to seek attention, but in faith give my wife attention—meeting her needs and trusting that he would meet my need for attention. I stepped out in faith and made that love choice. And amazingly, an overwhelming sense that he loved me expelled my fear just as Scripture promised: "Such love has no fear, because perfect love expels all fear" (1 John 4:18).

So after my faith choice to trust God to meet my need, I focused on Dottie first in my conversations. When I would talk to her after a speaking engagement I would first ask about how her day went. Sometimes I had to pry a little to get her to share first. I would ask about the kids and get them on the phone to find out how their day went too. I have to admit that sometimes the conversation about Dottie and the kids took so long that there wasn't much time for them to hear what was going on with me. But I placed my trust in God to meet my need for attention by being other-focused first. The amazing thing is that even when I had only a few minutes to share about my world, it felt great. The "little" attention I got from them became satisfying attention because I gave first and trusted God to meet my needs. And he did.

Being a fantastic lover does mean you give to another. You may fear in giving up your interests that you won't get your own needs met. But your love choices aren't about denying your needs so much as they are about your faith in a God who loves you and will meet your needs in his good time. And he won't fail you. Do you remember King David from the Old Testament? He's the one who committed adultery with Bathsheba. It is very interesting what God said to him after he lusted and had sex with another man's wife.

"I gave you your master's house," God said, "and his wives and the kingdom of Israel and Judah. And if that had not been enough, I would have given you much, much more. Why, then, have you despised the word of the LORD and done this horrible deed?" (2 Samuel 12:8-9). Essentially, God was telling David he had given him what he needed to meet his relational and sexual needs and would have even given more if he had thought that wasn't enough. But David's self-centeredness led him to fear his sex life wouldn't be fulfilling, so he took another man's wife. His first sin wasn't adultery—it was in a lack of faith in God his Provider. David didn't trust in him to meet his needs. His love choice would have been to trust in God's loving provision as his ultimate Provider. David eventually saw that and said, "I have sinned against the Lord" (2 Samuel 12:13).

Our fear-based self-centeredness is addressed when we trust in God that he will be our ultimate Provider and meet all our needs. Make that choice a consistent part of your life and you will become a fantastic lover.

There is another dimension to being a great lover that involves another love choice. It's true you need to know what love is and how to overcome your inclinations to be self-reliant and self-centered. But what is it that creates that deep intimate bond between two people? What causes a person to feel relationally intimate and what can you do to make that a continuing reality? That is the subject of the next part of this book.

5

I Choose to Love You by
Being a Fantastic Lover, Part 2

His breathing was slow and regular. He had never experienced such a deep sleep. It must have taken Adam a number of minutes to awaken and shake off God's anesthesia. And when he did finally gain his consciousness, imagine how he might have responded to what God had fashioned out of his rib.

Remember, Adam was created first. He lived in a perfect world where there was no sin. This first human enjoyed a perfect relationship with his Creator. This was paradise. God had masterfully made everything and yet in the midst of this perfect and sinless world, he had declared, "It is not good…" (Genesis 2:18).

What was not good? Surely God would not have created something that wasn't good. But he declared that something wasn't yet complete, and it would not be good to leave it incomplete. This incompletion was Adam's aloneness. "It is not good for the man to be alone. I will make a helper who is just right for him" (Genesis 2:18). So imagine with me. Adam wakes to find this creature called woman, created to remove the aching aloneness that God had placed deep within him.

Imagine him gazing through softly waving palms to see a face so captivating that he thought he'd be content never to look at anything else again. He is momentarily stunned as she emerges from a shroud of mist, moving toward him without hesitation. Her physical appearance excites him like nothing ever has. He is in awe of this creature. He has never experienced such beauty.

Their physical attraction must have been immediate and their sexual encounter must have been incredible. But Adam was intrigued by more than just Eve's glorious body. There was a certain mystery to his attraction. There was something alluring about Eve, as if he needed something she had—something he was missing. He sensed an indefinable hunger to know more of this creature than what he could physically hold and caress and enjoy. And so did she. They were both drawn to deeper attraction than their physical senses could experience.

Each of these first humans had a desire to know something about the other beyond what they could see with their eyes or touch with their physical bodies. They experienced a longing for an emotional connection, a bonding of the inner being, a deepening attachment of the soul. In short, they experienced a desire for intimacy—a desire to have their aloneness removed. They and every human born after them have sought that sense of closeness, connectedness, openness, transparency, and oneness with another person. We all need someone in our lives to remove our aloneness.

If we were created by God to enjoy such intimacy, then what do we do to experience it? What causes a person to feel relationally intimate with another? What is it that removes our relational aloneness? Is it something we do or something we say or simply something we're struck by out of nowhere—like Cupid's arrow? Actually, I don't think it is so much something we work hard at saying or doing so much as it is something we pursue. In other words, to discover the connectedness we all long for, we must engage in a pursuit of intimacy. And the Bible gives us some wonderful insights on how to do that.

Choosing to Know Your Lover

My friend Dr. David Ferguson introduced me to three Old Testament Hebrew words that help us to understand how to pursue relational intimacy. He outlines this in his superb marriage book *Never Alone*.

The first word is *yada*, which means "to know." God said, "I knew you before I formed you in your mother's womb" (Jeremiah 1:5). He knows you intimately. He is thoroughly and deeply acquainted with you. He knows your thoughts, your inclinations, your talents, gifts, motivations, aspirations, and dreams. He has explored the innermost recesses of your mind and heart and is intimately acquainted with who you are.

I believe God has created each one of us with the need to be deeply known by others. It's as if he permanently planted a sign on us that says, "Please know me." Our desire to be loved, really loved, is this cry for someone to discover who we are and love and accept what they find. Being known by another person removes a portion of our aloneness.

One of my friends, Mark, once told me he loved his wife but his marriage had grown dull and stale. He explained he was going through the motions of doing the right things and saying the right things. His wife, Susan, said in turn that she loved Mark but the spark was gone out of their relationship.

Mark said he had gone about as far as he could in knowing his wife. "I know about everything there is to know about Susan," he said, "and she's not as interesting to me as she once was." Of course he was wrong. He hadn't even scratched the surface of understanding the unique complexities of his wife. Not one of us has ever explored the true depths of the personality and character of our spouse or lover. King David wrote that God "made all the delicate, inner parts of my body and knit me together in my mother's womb. Thank you for making me so wonderfully complex!" (Psalm 139:13-14). Not only our bodies but our minds and hearts are complex.

Fortunately Mark came to his senses and realized he didn't understand and know Susan as he thought he did. Something Susan shared sparked his interest, and he began to explore aspects of her personality and character that he had yet to discover. He began to pursue truly knowing her. He later told me, "I was so blind to Susan's complexity. I thought I understood her, Josh, but I didn't. It will take a lifetime and beyond to know the woman I love. It's like I've fallen in love all over again."

What Mark discovered was that there is clearly a mystery in loving a spouse, and this mystery is designed by God. Count on it, you don't *really* know the person you love. Sure, you may know her favorite flavor of ice cream, his favorite color, her taste in music, or the sports team he's crazy about. But there is a depth and complexity to your spouse that when discovered reveals a fascinating and intriguing dimension of his or her life that is yet to be loved.

When I was first married, I loved Dottie—there was no question about that. Yet there were many relational aspects about her I didn't know or understand back then, and she is still largely a mystery to me today. That is the way God designed us. Our immense complexity keeps us from being relationally known by others unless a person uncovers our relational needs layer by layer. It is by this uncovering process that our distinct and unique relational characteristics are discovered. It is this mystery that drives my pursuit of intimacy with my wife, and it is what keeps our relationship fresh and exciting.

This is a simple thing, but for years and years when Dottie shared a problem or struggle or a hurt she was feeling, I thought she was looking for me to "fix it." I seemed to always have a plan of action that I thought solved her problem. The real problem was that I didn't understand her deeply enough to know what she needed at that particular moment. What I had to say may have helped a little, but it wasn't what she really needed at that specific moment. The apostle Paul tells us to give helpful words "according to the need of the moment, so that it will give grace to those who hear" (Ephesians

4:29 NASB). In my pursuit of intimacy I needed to discover my wife's relational needs and how to meet them. And when I did I removed a portion of her aloneness.

One day Dottie came home from a meeting at school very hurt over what some mothers had said about one of our kids. In the past when she shared a problem like that with me, I would leap on the situation and say something like, "Honey, don't let it get to you. Here's what you need to do." Then I would outline a plan to fix the problem. It may have been a good plan, but it didn't address the pain she felt at the moment. I was discovering, slowly but surely, what Dottie needed at those moments. As she shared her hurt I slipped over and simply put my arms around her and said, "Honey, I'm so sorry that you had to hear those words. I hurt for you, I love you." That was it—no fix-it plan, no corrective measures outlined, just a heartfelt expression that identified with her pain.

Amazingly, that was all Dottie needed right then. What was I learning? I was learning to know my wife relationally. She needed to be heard, not solved. I was coming to understand that when she feels grief or woundedness she needs comforting words and an affirming embrace rather than a pep talk or a fix-it plan. A few days later she came back to me and asked what I thought she could do to address those critical comments about the family member. My fix-it plan was then useful.

Do you see what happened when I discovered my wife's relational need of the moment and moved in to meet that need? I was removing some of her aloneness, and that resulted in greater intimacy between us. When we come to know more deeply the one we love and are open to meet his or her relational needs, it results in relational intimacy.

Again, the Bible gives us such insights about relationally knowing another person and how being present to them actually meets their "need of the moment." Jesus said, "A new command I give you: Love one another. As I have loved you, so you must love one another"

(John 13:34 NIV). At least 35 times in the New Testament, we see this recurring word pattern—an action verb followed by the words "one another." Scripture then goes on to give us specific instructions on how to love "one another"—to know another person deeply enough to meet their relational need of the moment.

Now here's the amazing thing. The person you love is so uniquely crafted that in all probability his or her relational needs are on different levels of priority than yours. In 1 Corinthians 12:25 it says to care for (give attention) to one another, and in 2 Thessalonians 5:11 it says to encourage one another. The person you love may have a very high need for attention and a lower need for encouragement. On the other hand, you may feel a high need for a lot of encouragement but not need much attention. It really all depends on your personal characteristics and your past experiences, such as the kind of home life you experienced.

Again, I need to credit my friend David Ferguson for introducing me to these "one anothers" of Scripture and explaining how to identify your top relational needs in order of priority. This is so valuable. Know your spouse's top ten needs in order of priority and it will do wonders in your pursuit of intimacy.

In the appendix of this book I have provided you with David's "Relational Needs Assessment Inventory." It is a testing tool to determine what relational needs are most dominant in your life. Take the test and ask the one you love to take it as well to share the priorities of your relational needs with each other. It's interesting to try to guess before the test which of the ten your spouse's most dominant needs are. You might be surprised.

Now, let's take a look at ten relational needs identified in Scripture and how to meet them. This will allow you to better know the person you love and help you remove a little of his or her aloneness. The result will be a greater intimacy. To start off the discussion of these relational needs, I will state how the person you love might feel when you step in to meet each need.

The Relational Need for Comfort

I feel comforted when you grieve with me when I hurt.
When you identify with a measure of my pain I feel closer to you.
(See 2 Corinthians 1:3-4.)

Scripture says to "mourn with those who mourn" (Romans 12:15 NIV). When you do this with your loved one who is hurting emotionally or physically, something extraordinary takes place. God "comforts us in all our troubles so that we can comfort others. When they are troubled, we will be able to give them the same comfort God has given us" (2 Corinthians 1:4). What happens when you give your spouse comfort? God is actually working through you to supernaturally provide comfort and emotional healing for his or her hurt.

I can testify that a fix-it plan isn't what is needed when your spouse is hurting. A response like, "In my opinion, dear, the reason this happened is…" doesn't work because the need of the moment is comfort. Comfort sounds more like, "I'm sorry this happened to you."

A teaching session isn't what is needed. A response like, "In these situations, God instructs us to…" won't do because the need of the moment is comfort. Comfort looks more like a tender hug.

A pep talk isn't what is needed. A response like, "Come on, honey, cheer up! The sun will come out tomorrow…" doesn't cut it because the need of the moment is comfort. Comfort sounds more like, "This must be so difficult for you."

Sound advice isn't what is needed. A response like, "If I were you, the next time this happens I would…" isn't really going to help because the need of the moment is comfort. Comfort sounds more like, "I so hurt with you right now."

Problem solving, teaching sessions, pep talks, and sound advice have their place and time, but not when your loved one is hurting. Because only comfort eases the pain. When you realize what he or she needs and you provide comfort, you are removing a little of his or her hurt and aloneness. And that increases your relational intimacy.

Let me also caution you on this one, especially the men. Don't think you have to understand exactly what another person is going through in order to comfort him or her. A friend of mine found out the hard way.

Once when his wife was at a very low point emotionally, he tried to help her, saying, "Honey, I know just what you're going through." She snapped back angrily, "No, you don't! How dare you say you know what I'm going through?" My friend was speechless, but his wife was right. To share in a spouse's sorrow does not mean that we necessarily know what he or she is going through. We cannot always participate in our spouse's unique experience. Rather, it means that because we know that he or she is hurting, we *hurt* with him or her. Our love causes us to identify with the one we love who is feeling pain. My friend should have said, "Honey, what you're going through must be tough, and I want you to know that I hurt with you." That way we identify with the pain of a spouse without giving the impression that we know exactly how he or she feels—which he or she knows is not true. Know the one you love—understand that meeting the need for comfort removes a measure of aloneness.

The Relational Need for Acceptance

I feel accepted when you love me without conditions, especially when my actions have been less than perfect. When you accept me for who I really am, blemishes and all, I feel closer to you.
(See Romans 15:7.)

Many couples get acceptance and approval confused. Just because we can't approve of someone's performance doesn't mean we can't accept him or her for who he or she is as a person. True acceptance separates the actions of a spouse from the core of who that spouse is—a person whom you have chosen to love for better or for worse.

We are all imperfect beings and need to know that what we do or don't do isn't going to destroy the relationship we have with our spouse. Acceptance is the need to know that regardless of your mistakes, you are loved anyway. Even if nothing were ever to change about you, you would still want to feel secure that you are wanted and loved. That is what your spouse wants as well. When your spouse receives that kind of acceptance, it removes a little of his or her aloneness, and he or she begins to experience intimacy with you.

The Relational Need for Attention (Care)

I feel cared for when you enter my world
and demonstrate your interest and concern.
(See 1 Corinthians 12:25.)

We live in a fast-paced world. You and the one you love may have different jobs, different friends, and a different set of personal interests. It's not difficult to feel overlooked or unimportant in the hectic and hurried routines of life. During those times you and your lover probably feel the need for attention.

You give attention to another person when you enter his or her world, learn what is important to him or her, and become involved in that world. Attention can be expressed like this: "Tell me about your day. I'm interested in what happened with your latest project." Any time you express interest in what's going on in a person's life or willingly get involved in doing what he or she wants to do, you are meeting the need for attention—and such action draws you closer to that person.

The Relational Need for Approval

I feel approved of when you express satisfaction with me
as a person and demonstrate you are pleased with me.
(See Romans 14:18.)

We all need to be affirmed that we are of worth. Rather than showing approval for what your spouse has accomplished, focus more on why he or she has accomplished it. This places the value on your spouse's character and lets him or her know you approve not only of what has been accomplished but also of the quality of the person who accomplished it.

Approval expresses itself with words like, "I'm so impressed with you as a host to our friends tonight. Your ability to create such a warm and inviting atmosphere is amazing." Or, "The yard looks great. Your attention to details shines through and makes our place look fantastic. I'm so proud of you." When you express approval to the one you love for what has been done as well as the qualities it took to accomplish it, you remove a little more of his or her aloneness, and you grow closer together.

The Relational Need for Support

*I feel support when you come alongside me to help
lift my load and help carry one of my struggles or problems.*
(See Galatians 6:2.)

Being supportive can be represented in physical or material things like pulling down the Christmas decorations from the attic, moving furniture, washing the car, weeding the garden, washing the dishes, and so on. Support is when you come alongside someone and help carry the load. Support can also share the load of relational or emotional burdens such as dealing with a difficult colleague at your spouse's work, making a financial decision, or responding to a child's need for discipline and guidance. Support is being available to carry a burden together.

Support sounds something like, "I want to be there for you and help. What can I do to lift your load right now?" Sometimes support is demonstrated in things you can do for or with your spouse. Other times it is being there to listen and care about what is going on in his or her life at the moment. When you are being supportive you draw closer to the person you love and alleviate some of his or her aloneness.

The Relational Need for Appreciation

*I feel appreciated when you praise me and communicate
gratefulness for one of my accomplishments or efforts.*
(See 1 Corinthians 11:2.)

When you accept another person for who he or she is, it says "Your *being* matters." When you express your appreciation, it says "Your *doing* matters." It gives the one you love a sense of significance—a feeling that he or she is valued and that what he or she does makes a difference to you. It conveys the idea *Hey, I'm worth something to someone!*

Praise is one of the best ways to show appreciation. A heartfelt "Thank you!" can be so meaningful at times: "Thank you, dear, for that great meal." "Thank you for making me feel so special tonight." "Thank you for helping me clean out the car." Praising your spouse is even more meaningful when it is done in front of others. Let your kids, in-laws, and friends hear you praise your spouse. It will remove a little of his or her aloneness and create a deeper sense of intimacy between you.

The Relational Need for Respect

*I feel respected when you value my thoughts and ideas
and consider me a person of worth.*
(See 1 Peter 12:10.)

We all have a need to feel valued and be recognized as a person of worth. Respect acknowledges that value and worth and lifts up another person. Your spouse will feel respected when you value his or her ideas, opinions, desires, or even personal space. You demonstrate respect when you seek out his or her perspective on an issue or find out how he or she feels about a matter.

Different people feel respected in various ways. Your husband may feel highly respected when his views are sought out. Your wife may feel more respected when her schedule is honored by your being on time and by your protecting her private time or space. Respect is communicated most effectively when it aligns with what a person values. If a husband is a creative thinker he may feel more respected when his wife seeks out his thinking on x, y, or z. If a wife is good with money matters, she will feel more respected when her husband stays within the family budget. However it is done, when you show respect to the one you love, it draws you closer, both emotionally and relationally.

The Relational Need for Affection

I feel close to you when you communicate care for me
through endearing words and physical touch.
(See Romans 12:10.)

We were created with the capacity and need to feel loved through affectionate words and a tender touch. A gentle touch and warm embrace say, "You're lovable." Meeting your spouse's need for affection can help you stay connected emotionally.

Some people have a higher need for affection than others. I knew of a man who obsessively held his wife's hand or had his arm around her almost all the time in a rather stifling manner. Touch is what communicated love to him, so he wanted to be in affectionate contact with his wife almost all the time. Yet his wife didn't find his touchy-feely approach all that meaningful. Oddly enough, his excessive touching worked against his need for affection because she didn't return the favor.

When you sensitively recognize your spouse is receptive to affectionate words and touch, take the initiative to meet his or her need for affection. Such affection can build the emotional closeness that enriches sexual intimacy, or on other occasions it can be just as meaningful to enjoy a romantic walk or share a quiet evening together listening to music or watching a TV program.

The Relational Need for Encouragement

I feel encouraged by you when you inspire me and
urge me forward to a positive goal.
(See Hebrews 10:24.)

Disappointment, discouragement, and frustration are a part of life. At such times we need to be encouraged, especially when we have lost sight of a goal or when we are not meeting some expectation. We receive encouragement when someone inspires us, lifts our spirits, and gives us hope.

One of the best ways to be an encouragement to another is by expressing confidence in him or her. Saying something like, "I know this particular time is tough, but I believe in you," can be of great encouragement. You can even meet your spouse's need of encouragement by providing a diversion. "How about going out to eat and taking in a fun movie?"

When your loved one feels down and discouraged, the need of the moment is encouragement. As you caringly and sensitively move in to lift his or her spirits, you remove a little of the aloneness, and you experience a deeper sense of togetherness and intimacy.

The Relational Need for Security

I feel secure when you take steps to remove the fear of loss
or want in my life. When you let me know that no matter
what, our relationship is solid, I feel secure.
(See 1 John 4:18.)

All the needs we have identified so far are related to the immediate moment. The need for security, however, focuses more on a need about the future. We can feel satisfied when our immediate need for encouragement, affection, or acceptance is met. We can feel safe and protected from physical danger or deprivation in the present. But we also need to be free from the fear of danger in the future. And we feel secure when we are confident that we will be taken care of in the future.

You can give your spouse a sense of physical and material security in the way you handle your finances and plan for your future together. You can provide emotional and relational security through your faithfulness and commitment to the relationship. In various ways you can communicate the sentiment that "I love you now, and no matter what I will always love you." Meeting your spouse's need for security deepens your relational connection and intimacy.

Knowing your lover and meeting the need of the moment will result in relational intimacy. Make your pursuit of intimacy an intentional one—move in to meet his or her need for comfort, acceptance, attention, approval, appreciation, support, respect, affection, encouragement, and security. It will pay huge dividends. But as important as it is to know your spouse, it is equally important to allow him or her to know you.

Choosing to Allow Your Lover to Know You

Chad was a hardworking man, putting in long hours at the office. When he came home he wanted to leave his work behind. He said he didn't have much to talk about with Leslie, his wife, except her work. So the conversations mostly revolved around Leslie, how she felt, what she was dealing with at work, and their two elementary-age children.

Leslie was glad that Chad was a good listener, and she felt he loved her. But she explained, "I've been married to Chad for ten years now, and I really don't feel close to him. It's like he won't let me into his life. It's not that he's secretive or anything. He just doesn't share his feelings with me."

Chad claims he's not trying to be closed, but that he's not comfortable sharing himself emotionally. He says, "I guess I'm not a touchy-feely kind of guy. I don't like talking about my feelings."

Some people are hesitant to open up and share what they are thinking and feeling. That's understandable. You need to be careful with whom you share your deep feelings because some people cannot be trusted and you could get emotionally wounded. But that should not be the case with your spouse. And unless you are able to overcome those hesitancies, your caution will keep you from experiencing relational intimacy in marriage. Intimacy not only enables you to get to know the one you love, but also it enables him or her to know you in a deep and sustaining friendship.

King Solomon said the Lord "offers his friendship to the godly" (Proverbs 3:32). Friendship in this verse is the Hebrew word *sod*, meaning "vulnerable or transparent disclosure." In other words, God offers his friendship—a transparent disclosure of himself—to the godly. He has revealed himself to us through his Son, Jesus, and also through his Holy Spirit. He wants us to know him so he can have an intimate relationship with us.

If you are to be a successful lover you must learn to open yourself up, disclose yourself, and be vulnerable. That is not always easy to do, especially for people like Chad who grew up with a verbally and emotionally abusive father. His dad told him what he was to think and how he was to feel. He wasn't allowed to freely express how he felt, so he "learned" to suppress his feelings at a young age. Today he finds it hard to even know what he feels, let alone express it.

Opening up and being transparent about your dreams, aspirations, hopes, and expectations may be risky, and at times you may even get emotionally hurt. But it is a risk worth taking.

If you are hesitant to be vulnerable with your spouse or loved one, start by being transparent about your fear. Share that it scares you to be too open and then explain why. Allow your spouse to probe the sources of those fears. Bring your fears to the surface and into the light. And if you are the one who is helping your spouse reveal his or her fears, you have a very important role to play. You can alleviate those fears by being a safe and unconditionally accepting lover. Remember, the Bible says that "perfect love expels all fear" (1 John 4:18).

Your pursuit of intimacy goes both ways. It involves you pursuing the depth of the person you love by knowing who he or she is—with hopes, joys, fears, and relational needs. It also means opening up yourself to be known by being transparent and revealing who you really are—your hopes, joys, fears, and relational needs. Together this knowing and being known remove aloneness and create relational intimacy.

However, there is yet another dimension to intimacy. It has to do with choosing to journey together with another person.

Choosing to Be Caringly Involved in Your Lover's Life

King David wrote, "O LORD, you have examined my heart and know everything about me...Every moment you know where I am" (Psalm 139:1-3). The Hebrew word *sakan*, translated "know" here, means a caring involvement. God's knowing of David was much more than superficial and informational; he was caringly involved in David's life.

Being caringly involved in the life of your lover results in deepened relational intimacy. It means choosing to enter your spouse's world and journey with him or her in what he or she is involved in and interested in.

I mentioned earlier that I made a choice to hear from Dottie first when I would call home. Rather than dominating the conversation with what was going on in my life, I wanted to hear from her. What I was actually choosing to do was to be caringly involved in Dottie's life—her world. You see, she and I lived in two literally different worlds. She lived at home with the kids and had the day-to-day responsibilities of rearing our family. I lived on the road speaking night after night in cities all over the country. This arrangement could have destroyed our relationship had we not chosen to be caringly involved in each other's life.

Because we chose to journey with each other through life, Dottie and I experienced a deepened relational intimacy. We shared in the responsibility of raising our kids together. Sure, it was more challenging that I was gone a lot. But the various decisions we made, we made together. We also shared the ministry accomplishments and struggles. Dottie entered my ministry world and felt the joys and challenges with me. Our journey became a grand adventure. It still is.

You live a busy life. It seems the more technology you take advantage of to make life easier, the busier life becomes. And in all your busyness, if you're not careful, life's pressures can make your focus all about you and what you're facing. Resist this tendency and choose to be caringly involved in the world of the person you love. As you do, you will become a better lover—a lover who knows what relational intimacy is all about.

Choose to know the person you love—really know him or her. Discover the dreams, hopes, fears, and joys of his or her life. Understand his or her relational needs and move in to meet those needs. Choose to allow your lover to know you. Open up, be vulnerable, and share who you are—your hopes, dreams, joys, and fears. Be transparent about your relational needs and allow your lover to move into your life and meet those needs. And finally, choose to enter the world of your lover and be caringly involved in his or her interests. Make those interests your own and journey through life together. This is the proven way to relational intimacy. This is truly the secret to loving.

6

I Choose to Love You by
Becoming a Great Listener

What would you say is the most common marital problem today? What do you think substantially improves relationships and increases relational intimacy? If you had to name only one issue that plagues or assists couples the most, what would that be?

If you said communication, healthy communication, you would be right. Conventional wisdom and research say healthy communication is a predictor of a healthy relationship. And the cornerstone to healthy communication is the ability to become a great listener.

If we listened as much as we talked, healthy communication would begin to take care of itself. The apostle James wrote, "Be quick to listen, slow to speak" (James 1:19). The phrase "quick to listen" means to be "a ready listener." To become a great listener is to be alert—ready to hear what another person wants to say. Someone has said that because God gave us two ears and one mouth we should listen twice as much as we talk.

Healthy communication is a process, either verbal or nonverbal, of exchanging information with another person so that other person understands what you are communicating. That involves at least three key ingredients: talking, listening, and understanding. In this chapter I want to concentrate on the listening ingredient of healthy communication.

A lot of people think talking—with the goal of getting their point of view across—is communication. Healthy communication, however, requires both talking *and* listening. If there is no true listening, understanding and deepened intimacy simply can't happen.

Think for a moment about what you bring to a relationship as a natural result of who you are. What does your spouse bring to the relationship? You each bring a unique background and style of communication from your family of origin and the culture of your childhood and adolescence. Two different lifestyles, catalogs of experience, and personal histories are being blended. Unless each of you is able to listen carefully enough to identify those things the other is simply assuming that everyone thinks, it will be difficult to achieve a satisfying level of communication and intimacy. Good listening is about understanding what another person is saying and meaning. It is about appreciating the other person's point of view. That doesn't mean you necessarily agree with the point of view, but you have clearly heard it.

You may say, "I hear you, but being a good listener doesn't come naturally to me." I'm not sure it comes naturally to any of us. Listening is a learned art—and you can learn to listen. I am living proof of that.

When Listening Speaks Volumes

When either of you fails to listen effectively to the other, frustration can set in. It can lead to a breakdown in the relationship if not dealt with quickly. As I have confessed, I have been guilty of talking too much and not listening enough in the early years of our marriage.

About seven or eight months after Dottie and I were married, she came to me rather hesitantly. I could tell she was hurting. "I don't think you love me," she confessed.

"What!" I exclaimed. "You've got to be kidding! I love you more than anyone else on the face of this earth."

"Honey," she replied, "I really don't think you are interested in some of the areas of my life that interest me. I don't think you care about some of the 'little' areas."

Ouch! That was like driving a knife through my heart. Immediately I asserted, "But I do too!"

I was amazed as Dottie explained why she felt that way. "You never listen to me. I will start to share something with you, and you will cut me off or change the subject. Or, I will start to share something with you, and your mind is off somewhere else. You often pretend you're listening, but your mind is on a free-speech platform in Bolivia." That's my wife's way of saying, "Darling, you're thinking about something else while I'm talking to you."

One indicator of a healthy relationship is emergence of little phrases that are meaningful only to the couple. I won't share all of the ones Dottie and I have, but when she wants me to know that I'm looking at her but thinking of something else, she'll ask, "Are you on a platform in Bolivia?" (I got my start doing free-speech debates with Marxists in Latin America.)

You know what I discovered was happening? Because I had never learned to listen to people, I was unintentionally communicating to my wife that I didn't care, and she was starting to retreat into a shell.

I was listening to Dottie's words, but I really didn't hear the message she was conveying. Listening to words and hearing your loved one's message are two different things. When we hear the words but miss the message, it seems as if we don't care about the value of our loved one.

Since I had not made a concerted effort (and sometimes made no effort at all) to listen to Dottie, I was communicating to her that what she had to say wasn't important. What a way to strangle a partner's enthusiasm! Really listening says to another person, *You are important! You are of great value!* Respect begins with listening.

Listening is one of the most profound ways to show other people that you take them seriously; that you care; that you value their opinions.

Dr. David Augsburger, senior professor of pastoral care and counseling in the School of Theology at Fuller Theological Seminary, wrote *Caring Enough to Hear and Be Heard*. This book, written over thirty years ago, is just as relevant today as it was then. The subtitle of his book is *How to Hear and Be Heard in Equal Communication*. Dr. Augsburger relates effective listening to a person's sense of worth:

- If you listen to me, then I must be worth hearing.
- If you ignore me, I must be a bore.
- If you approve of my views or values, then I have something of worth to offer.
- If you disapprove of my comment or contribution, then I apparently had nothing to say.
- If I cannot be with you without using your comments for self-evaluation, then leveling will be impossible. If I am preoccupied with what you think of me, then I have already shut you out.[1]

Go Beyond Hearing to Listening

Have you ever said to someone, "You're not listening to me," only to have him or her say, "Oh yes, I am," and then repeat the last sentence you just spoke? As you recognize when you hear that, it is one thing to *hear* and quite another thing to *listen*.

We might say when you are trying to hear something that you are attempting to gain content. It's like when you're watching the football halftime show and say, "Pipe down, kids, I want to hear the scores." You are really saying that you're seeking information for your own purposes. Listening is different. Listening is focused on the person who is talking—caring about what he or she is saying. Hearing is more concerned about what *you* want out of the conversation. Listening is more about trying to understand the feelings and position of the other person. Hearing tends to be focused on you; listening tends to be focused on others.

There are also various levels of listening. In his book, Dr. Augsburger goes on to relate each level (or attitude and intent) to its care for the other person.

> One can listen for facts, data, details to use for one's own end or to quote for other purposes, and so offer no caring at all.

> Or one can listen out of sympathy that is energized by pity. To be nourished by one's own pitying is to feed one's pride on the pain of others. To be moved by pity to care is a far different thing. Simple sympathy may not be caring at all.

> Or one can listen as another ventilates about a person not present and actually increase the pain and distance between them by implying, through listening, that gossiping about absent others is useful talk. It's not caring at all.

> Or one can listen out of apathy or obligation or professional habit or simple niceness, and give no real caring to the other. To care is more than to offer an ear. Habitual hearing may not be caring after all.

> Or one can listen inquisitively, with the curiosity of a voyeur peering in at another's private zones. To care is more than to offer wide eyes. The eager ear or eye may not care at all.

> Or one can listen "helpfully" as a rescuer with ready first aid, inserting support, understanding, reassurance at each pause. To care is to both give and withhold help. Being chronically helpful may be no help at all.

> Yet caring includes elements of each of the above. Accurate attention to what is said, a genuine empathy, a willingness to stand with another when he or she is saying

things that are exaggerated through stress, a disinterest that allows objectivity, a willingness to see the other as he or she is, a commitment to be truly helpful as the moment for useful help arrives—all these are ingredients in real care, but they are clarified and corrected by the central element of caring.[2]

Caring, then, is a critical part of our listening. A caring heart reaches out through a listening ear. And that should include some verbal or body language feedback. Silence can even be a good response if it communicates nonverbal caring with some positive body language. The key is to give some form of feedback.

One wife, hurt and frustrated by a total lack of response from her husband, was heard to exclaim, "If you're listening to me, respond! Say something. Say anything. Just let me know that you're listening to me!" When we reach out to others, we yearn for acknowledgment.

Here are some helpful suggestions to show that you are absorbing what your loved one is saying:

- *React physically.* Turn toward the person. Lean forward. Nod your head in response. Keep looking the person in the eye. Nothing shows greater interest than eye contact.

- *Request more information.* Ask a question that seeks clarification or additional details: "What did you mean by that?" Or, "Why is that important to you?" In asking questions you are saying, "Tell me more—I'm interested, I care."

- *Reflect on what has been said* with a leading statement: "You seem quite excited about meeting him." Or, "That must have been rough on you." Reflective listening pays off in more intimate sharing.

- *Repeat or rephrase statements with feeling.* Echoing the meaning or feeling of a statement both clarifies and encourages further communication.

- *Remain silent when he or she is telling a story.* Don't interrupt, and don't finish sentences for a person. This is a hard one for me. I have to keep telling myself, *Don't interrupt, don't interrupt.* Also, don't rush to fill a pause in the conversation simply to avoid the silence—you may cut off something important your loved one was preparing to share.

  Dottie admits, "Sometimes it frustrates me a little when Josh chimes in on my story. I feel like, *Doesn't he think I can tell the story myself, or does he think I'm going into too much detail, or what?* Other times I realize that it's merely a reflection of his enthusiasm. He gets excited about what I'm going to tell him, and he just jumps in—he doesn't see it as an intrusion or an interruption, or that he is taking anything away from me. I know he wants to join me in what I'm saying, but the best thing for me in sharing my feelings is when Josh lets me tell the story." Patience is a blessing.

- *Refrain from concentrating on your answer* or rebuttal while a person is still talking—it makes you impatient to speak. When you are constantly constructing a rebuttal or a way to justify something you've said, you are merely building up a defense. As a result you are not truly listening.

- *Express your encouragement and appreciation* for what a person has been sharing. Both of these enhance healthy communication. Solomon, in all his wisdom, knew that "kind words are like honey—enjoyable and healthful" (Proverbs 15:24). Say, "Thanks so much for sharing that. I'm sure it wasn't easy but I really appreciate it." Or, "What you've said makes a lot of sense, and I know it's going to help."

These responses are just a few of the ways to actively become a better listener. Remember that your ear can open the door to another's heart, so don't close it. Believe me, if you work on being a good listener, it will pay off.

Choose to become a great listener. It will take time, and it won't all come together at once. Let your spouse or loved one know you want to become a better listener, even a great one. Letting him or her know your intent is a great first step.

Becoming an excellent listener is foundational to healthy communication with the person you love. Learning to listen appropriately is vital; learning to talk with clarity is also an important part of learning the art of communication. Listening, talking, and understanding are the keys to effective communication. In the next chapter I'll focus on the art of talking and understanding to create healthy communications with the one you love.

7

COMMITMENT #5

I Choose to Love You by
Learning the Art of Communication

Oh, I forgot to mention it," I said to Dottie as we finished breakfast, "but Tim and Tammy just had their baby."

"Really, when?" Dottie asked.

"I'm not sure," I replied. "Yesterday, I think—maybe the day before."

"Was it a boy or a girl?"

"A boy, maybe," I said hesitantly. "No, I think it was a girl. Huh, I'm not sure."

Then the drill really began. "How much did the baby weigh?" "Beats me," I replied. "What did they name it?" "I don't know," I said, getting rather frustrated. "Is Tammy okay?" "I have no clue, Dottie," I replied shaking my head. "I'm sorry I ever brought it up!"

Hearing that a friend just had a new baby was satisfying enough for me. It was clear, however, that I certainly wasn't able to communicate adequately about it to my wife. I lacked the details. I needed to make an adjustment in the way I processed if I was to communicate effectively with Dottie.

"Think details!" became my motto. I started writing myself notes: "Josh, when you talk to Dottie you need to bring in details." After that I could hardly wait to talk to my wife after a friend had delivered a baby. "When?" "Last Tuesday." "How much did it weigh?" "Eight pounds." "Was it a boy or a girl?" "A girl." "What did they name her?" "Carla." And so forth. I worked to remember things I had never bothered with before, and it enhanced our marital communication because I was able to give Dottie the details—an important channel through which she feels connected to me. I still struggle with giving her details, but I will never give up working on it.

As I said in the last chapter, listening is the cornerstone to healthy communications, but your ability to talk is also critical. I guess that is why I'll never forget the day Dottie confronted me about my lack of details. She said kindly, but bluntly, "Honey, you don't talk right." I said, "I've talked like this my whole life!" "Well," she responded, "you're not communicating very clearly to me."

Dottie went on to point out how I never seemed to have the details. I have always been a big-picture guy with an interest in the "bottom line," so the details were never that important to me, but they were to her. As I made the necessary adjustment I was able to connect better and on a deeper level with my wife. For me it was the need to share more details—for you it might be something else. But what you say and how you say it are critical to communicating in a healthy way with the one you love. To help you in this area, I would like to share ten principles that have helped me become a better communicator. But before I do so, I want to address a common misconception about communication, especially marital communication.

I said earlier that conventional wisdom and research say healthy communication is a predictor of a healthy relationship. That's true, but that is not the same as saying that good communication produces good relationships. It's actually the other way around. People with good, emotionally connected relationships tend to communicate in a healthy manner. People in unhappy relationships tend to relate poorly to each other because of a connection problem—not because of a communication problem. When people are emotionally disconnected, communications tend to break down.

With that said, I suggest we think of the art of communication as an artfully designed channel for connecting emotionally and relationally with the person you love. That means the focus isn't on how to communicate better so much as it is about how to connect better. Healthy communication then becomes a means to an end—the end being a healthier relational connection to your lover. Healthy communication is other-focused; it's about connecting better and deepening the relationship.

Ten Principles of Artful Communication

Let's lay the ten principles of artful communication on the table. They are profoundly significant and practical. Put them into practice in your relationship and you will find they help to keep you connected with the one you love.

- Work at it.
- Learn to compromise.
- Seek to understand.
- Affirm your spouse's worth, dignity, and value.
- Be positive and encouraging.
- Practice confidentiality.
- Wait for the right time.
- Share your feelings sensitively.
- Avoid mind reading.
- Be honest.

1. Work at it. Doing what comes naturally may be the motto for many in our culture, but becoming a good communicator does not just happen naturally. All of us are affected by the self-reliance and self-centeredness of our lives, so we need to make a conscious effort based on a love choice to be other-focused. My choice was to go out of my way to listen to Dottie and let her know I was really interested in those areas that she found important. It did not come naturally to me—I had to work at it.

One of my habits was to read the newspaper at breakfast. I continued it early into our marriage. However, when Dottie reminded me that the breakfast table is a great place to talk, I gave it up. I never read a newspaper at the breakfast table again. I learned to cue myself as I walked to the table, *Now, Josh, remember. You're here to communicate with your wife this morning.* Today I have to be careful not to be using my iPhone and iPad at breakfast.

While on the road, I was quite sensitive to the cost of calling home. That was before unlimited minutes were available. But I began to realize that Dottie might have waited all day to share something with me—something that happened at home she wanted to talk about. However, being cost-conscious, I used to say, "This is long distance. Tell me when I get home."

This response shredded her motivation to open up and communicate. So I've had to learn to tell myself, *Josh, when Dottie answers, you are not going to mention the cost of this call. You are going to ask, "What's been happening today?" Then you will sit back and enjoy the conversation with your wife.* Back then, the calls were expensive, and they still are when I am traveling internationally, but they've been one of the best investments I have ever made in my marriage.

Learning the art of communication is work and will cost you time, energy, and perhaps even money. But because it provides a direct channel to relational intimacy and emotional connectedness with the one you love, it is well worth it.

2. Learn to compromise. A healthy marriage relationship is give and take, especially where differing styles of communicating are involved. Each person needs the freedom to be himself or herself while still adapting to the other's needs. One style isn't necessarily better than another. It's just that people are different when it comes to communication needs. A skillful communicator knows how and when to adjust.

Dottie and I have opposite needs for sharing details. Perhaps you can identify with the frequent frustration that can spawn. As Dottie puts it:

"Josh likes to get right to the point. He likes to know his facts. He wants the bottom line. I've been told I have a flair for the dramatic. Because of my personality I think telling a story should be a work of art—much like painting a picture. You don't approach an easel with a paint roller. You apply the details one at a time. So when telling a story, there is a stage to be set, a tone to be developed, and an atmosphere to be communicated.

"When Josh and I were first married, I think my style of communicating nearly drove him crazy. His body language would be screaming, 'Just get to the point!' And he would finally say, 'What's the point of the story?' And I would respond, 'Look, you're going to have to be patient and listen. It's my story. Please let me tell it my way.' Eventually he began to realize that details in a story were very important to me.

"I've also come to realize the essential place of compromise in a marriage. Now we both try to work at meeting each other's needs. He tries to remember more of the details and to be patient with me when I'm giving details to him. In turn, I try to spare him the agony of sitting through the extraneous. I try to summarize my message without the drama; to delete a lot of the details and get to the bottom line.

"How I informed Josh of my pregnancy with our third child is a good example of how I needed to compromise. After we had Kelly and Sean we both knew we wanted another child, but I became pregnant with Katie a bit earlier than we had anticipated. To give him the news, I made up a little poem that said in a roundabout way I was pregnant. It meant he had to listen all the way through to the very last line before he realized what it was getting at, and that it was about us.

"At the time we were living in Texas, and he was still involved in buying and selling antiques. He was traveling in California, and I happened to call him just five minutes before a big antique sale was to start. I said, 'I need to talk to you,' and he said, 'Okay, that's fine, but I don't have much time. They're getting ready to open the door and there are 500 people waiting to get in.' I told him I had something to read, and he agreed to listen as long as I read it fast.

"I started reading the poem, and he interrupted me in the middle and said, 'Wait a minute, whose poem is this?' I told him to be quiet for a minute and just listen carefully. Twice more he broke in as I was reading: 'Hold on, what are you talking about? Who is having a baby?' I just kept insisting, 'Don't say anything. You have to hear the whole poem.'

"Finally, at the end, he realized I was telling him *we* were going to have a baby. Now Josh would rather I had just stated the fact: 'I'm pregnant. We're going to have a baby in June.' But *I* had to go around the block, paint this picture, set the atmosphere, and make it very exciting—at least exciting for me. What I had to learn was that at times I couldn't communicate in my 'dramatic' sort of way and still be sensitive to my husband. I had to compromise. I should never have tried to read him my little poem over the phone, especially when he was about to go to an antique sale. I learned a valuable lesson that day, and I am still learning."

Dottie and I had to adapt our different styles of communicating to each other and make compromises. If you are going to communicate effectively with your spouse or loved one, you will need to adjust your style of communicating. Be sensitive and aware of how he or she processes and receives information, and then adjust accordingly.

3. Seek to understand. You've probably read the little placard, often on people's desks, that states, "I know you believe you understand what you think I said. But I am not sure you realize that what you heard is not what I meant." What you hear your loved one say is not necessarily what he or she meant. To bridge the difference between what is said and what is meant requires that you always seek to understand.

Do you first seek to be understood rather than seeking to understand the other person? Do you tend to listen with a hurried anticipation to reply? Do you sometimes decide prematurely what your loved one means before he or she is even finished talking? If so, you're not alone. I do it far more than I want to. When you and I do this, we may hear what another is saying, but we fail to understand what he or she really means.

Seeking to understand requires that we listen to get the perspective of the other person and see from his or her vantage point. This means we must apply Jesus' counsel to "do to others whatever you would like them to do to you" (Matthew 7:12). Therefore, we must seek to hear as we want to be heard and understand as we want to be understood.

4. Affirm your spouse's worth, dignity, and value. Each person has a deep need to be known and valued for who he or she is as a person of worth. When you seek to hear and understand your loved one's position and ideas and feelings, you are recognizing his or her worth to you. You may not agree with every point that is being made, but demonstrate that you respect and honor his or her position and view.

I see so many couples trying to change the other's views or consistently evaluating each other. More often than not these couples struggle to connect emotionally with each other, and their poor communications reflect it. When you affirm your spouse as a person of value you are saying, "You are worth listening to. Your thoughts matter to me." When he or she senses that affirmation, opening up and communicating effectively is easier.

Dottie tells me that one way she feels valued is when I praise her mind. "He's always telling me what a quick mind I have and how bright I am. At first I thought he was just saying those things to make me feel good. But over time he convinced me he really does value my input. He asks my opinion when he's editing books, films, or lectures. He's open to my perspective and especially interested in my sense about things intuitively. Those kinds of conversations are always interesting, and afterward I feel we are so much a part of each other."

I can assure you, this did not come naturally. What I learned was that I clearly needed Dottie's perspective in my life. She could hear things and see things I couldn't. She could hear tones in another person's voice I couldn't. She could feel things of the heart I couldn't quite sense. I needed her intuitive understanding of the people we met, the decisions we faced, various questions about raising our kids, and so on. I needed her insights, sensitivity, and wisdom about life. I know this sounds sentimental, but Dottie completes me. And because I have told her that repeatedly, our communication channels are much more open and clear.

But again, affirming my wife doesn't come naturally to me. Numerous times in our marriage Dottie has told me she hasn't felt needed. She has said, "You could run your entire life without me." I have never felt that way, and it has been hard to believe she could feel that. But it really doesn't matter what I have thought: if Dottie has felt that way, then her feeling tells me I have not communicated clearly how much I truly need her.

You need your spouse, perhaps more than you realize. If you sense your tendency is to be self-reliant, resist that tendency. You need the perspective, insight, and sensitivity only your spouse can give. That is one reason God brings a man and woman together. He has given each of us insights and abilities that the other needs, just as he has with his body, the church. "We are all parts of his one body," the apostle Paul said, "and each of us has a different work to do. And since we are all one body in Christ, we belong to each other, and each of us needs all the others" (Romans 12:5).

Husband, look to your wife and rely on her for her unique view of life. Let her know how valuable her insights are to you. Wife, look to your husband and depend on him for his different perspective on life. Let him know the value he brings to your life. As you both honor and value the other, your lines of communication will remain unobstructed and clear.

5. **Be positive and encouraging.** Being positive is a real plus factor in communication. It promotes openness with your spouse or loved one, whereas negativity tends to hinder healthy communication. It seems, though, that we naturally tend to accentuate the negative.

During a three-day lecture series at the University of Tennessee, I was in a meeting with the staff of a Christian campus organization and several key students. One young lady seemed particularly down and discouraged. She made this comment, "I'm not going to hand out any more flyers. Everybody's negative about the meetings we're sponsoring. All I've heard are negative reports this morning."

I immediately asked, "How many people have given you a hard time? Twenty-five?"

"No."

"Ten?"

"No."

"Was it five?" I asked.

Again she said, "No."

I discovered that only two people had reacted negatively to the two or three hundred flyers she had handed out. Everyone in the room, including her, realized she had accentuated the negative.

We tend to notice or remember the negative words or comments about ourselves when we encounter them in verbal or written communications. If ten positive statements and one negative statement are made, we will probably focus on the negative one most. The ratio of praise to criticism in a conversation would seem balanced if it consisted of a healthy 90 percent praise and 10 percent criticism.

Are you a positive communicator? It will be far easier for people to reach out to you and share if your orientation is positive. The apostle Paul gave excellent guidance about the proper emphasis of our attitude and lifestyle when he wrote, "Whatever is true, whatever is honorable, whatever is right, whatever is pure, whatever is lovely, whatever is of good repute, if there is any excellence and if anything worthy of praise, dwell on these things" (Philippians 4:8 NASB).

Encourage people and let your conversation be positive. Compare the following statements. Which one motivates you more?

- "You never give me flowers anymore."
- "I have so appreciated the times you have given me flowers."

Encouraging your spouse with positive remarks will almost always result in a positive response. Being sincerely grateful and uplifting to the one you love will go a long way toward maintaining healthy communication.

6. Practice confidentiality. What a plus factor it is in communication when your mate knows you are able to keep things to yourself. There's automatically a greater willingness for your loved one to be open with you when you practice confidentiality. In speaking I regularly use personal illustrations to amplify my points, but I must be very careful of what I share about my relationship with Dottie and our children. If I were to speak too openly about the intimacies of our relationship, Dottie inevitably would become cautious and defensive.

A young lady named Joyce asked to talk to me about her situation with Wendel. Wendel wanted the relationship to develop along more serious lines toward marriage and was pressing Joyce to define the extent of her commitment to him. Joyce wasn't quite sure of her feelings. In a long talk with Wendel she had shared how hesitant she was to make future commitments because of some personal areas she felt she needed to work through first.

Wendel, out of frustration, had gone to a number of people for advice. In seeking their input, he had shared what Joyce had confided in him. When this got back to Joyce, she became very defensive. She felt her privacy had been invaded, and understandably she was questioning if she could ever open up to him again.

Do you keep things to yourself? Or do you tend to tell others certain things about your love life "in confidence"? Publicly airing private matters destroys the trust in a relationship. When you or your loved one feels betrayed, it becomes much harder to be transparent the next time.

7. Wait for the right time. King Solomon was a wise man. "Timely advice," he said, "is lovely, like golden apples in a silver basket" (Proverbs 25:11). "It is wonderful to say the right thing at the right time!" (Proverbs 15:23). Healthy communication is far more apt to be achieved when the right words are spoken *at the right time*.

In relationships with a spouse, a friend, or with anyone, we must be sensitive not only about the way we speak but also to the timing. Depending upon the situation, it may be best to wait until morning to share something controversial with your spouse. This is especially true if he or she has had a very difficult day. Dottie explains her approach to timing this way: "I'm a very communicative person—it's important to me. And I've always wanted to have a relationship where we communicated about everything all of the time. I still do. But I learned early in our marriage that if I had something to tell Josh that was very important—a problem, something I was struggling with, or any heavy subject at all—I needed to choose carefully not only how I told him, but when.

"There are times when he doesn't want something heavy on his mind; like ten minutes before he gets up to speak (or maybe even the day of a talk). If there was a real problem with one of the children or if I was feeling hurt, I would hold off on telling him until the right time. When he was about to face a large audience, I didn't want to tell him things that could preoccupy his mind and diminish his effectiveness. Even now I avoid laying something heavy on him before he goes to bed because it can disrupt his sleep. So I wait until the morning."

Choose the right time, the right atmosphere, the right setting to explore issues that need thoughtful consideration or could trigger an emotional response. Saying the right things at the right time will help avoid stress in the relationship.

8. Share your feelings sensitively. Human emotions are a part of being human, yet some people find it difficult to share their feelings. Depending on childhood experiences, some people are not even in touch with their feelings. Yet if you and I are going to develop a deep and intimate relationship with another we must be able to communicate our feelings.

Expressing what you are feeling allows the one you love to know where you are at the moment and what you are going through. Allow him or her to know what you're truly feeling. Suppressing your feelings can be harmful to both you and your relationship. When you bury or suppress hurts, frustration, or anger, you don't eliminate them from your life. You actually bury them alive. And at some point they will emerge again, but not in a healthy way.

The key to healthy communication is to allow your loved one to know what you are feeling, even anger, but to do so in a sensitive way. The Bible says, "Don't sin by letting anger control you. Don't let the sun go down while you are still angry" (Ephesians 4:26). You don't gain control of your emotions by burying them or by letting them out insensitively. One safeguard is to name to your loved one what you're feeling but add that you don't want to say anything hurtful. I will sometimes say, "Dottie, I'm getting frustrated here, and I want to be sure I don't say anything to hurt you." This helps me realize I need to tread softly, and it alerts her to ease up a little bit and try to be more understanding. I've also had to learn to be careful how I say things. Rather than telling Dottie what I think and what offended me, I try to open up vulnerably and let her know, "Honey, this is what I'm feeling right now." (We will get into the area of how to express your feelings in depth in the chapter on resolving conflicts.)

When you express your feelings honestly and sensitively it not only allows your loved one to know you, it allows him or her to help you work through those feelings. It also avoids the problem of buried or unresolved feelings coming back to disrupt the relationship. Communicating your feelings sensitively makes for a healthy relationship.

9. Avoid expecting your spouse to read your mind. Warning: Don't take it for granted that the other person understands your gestures, the tone of your voice, or your body language. Frustration arises in a relationship when each person assumes the other knows what he or she is thinking and feeling. Mind-reading rarely works. You can't hold your spouse responsible for not responding to your hurts, needs, or feelings if you haven't said them out loud. Everyone needs to speak up!

"I take full blame for a conflict with Josh on our honeymoon," Dottie admits. "We were in Mexico and driving to Acapulco, which put us in the car together for several hours. I was a new bride and thought, 'I'm married to this man, but he doesn't know everything there is to know about me. I even have some close girlfriends that know more about me than my own husband does! Since we're married he should know everything about me.' (It didn't occur to me that we had a lifetime ahead of us to get acquainted.) So I thought I'd better tell him just how I felt about everything, so he could really know his wife.

"The time span between our first date and our marriage had been just over six months, so I knew there was a lot I hadn't been able to tell Josh in that short dating period. I was feeling the need to share, so I proceeded to talk and talk and talk while he watched for road signs and fumbled with maps. I should have known that a person couldn't absorb all I had to say in that short of time, but I expected him to catch everything I was saying. When I sensed he was not being very attentive or didn't give me much feedback, I began to clam up. At that point I thought he would know why I had stopped talking, but he didn't. In fact, he didn't even seem to notice I had shut down.

"As the clock ticked on in silence, I continued to grow angrier. The problem was, he had absolutely no idea what was going on in my mind. By the time we reached Acapulco I could hardly see straight. I got out of the car and told him I was furious. 'Why?' he asked. I said, 'Because you didn't even talk to me all the way down!' Josh didn't have the foggiest idea why I was fuming. I assumed he should know what I was feeling and thinking even though I didn't share it.

"I'm an intuitive person, and I can usually sense when another person is uncomfortable about something. I wouldn't say Josh is oblivious to how people feel, but he doesn't have a high intuitive sense. My problem was that it took me a long while to figure this out. In the meantime I was expecting my husband to read my mind on what I felt about things. Truth is, none of us are good mind-readers, and it inhibits healthy communications when you expect someone to read your mind."

10. Be honest. The Bible says, "Speak the truth in love" (Ephesians 4:15). We are to be honest with a person—speak the truth about them yet be sure to make the security, welfare, and happiness of that person as important as your own. In other words, healthy communication requires honest words and a caring heart.

Picture this: your wife gets a new hairstyle. She loves it, but you think it looks absolutely ridiculous. She comes into the room, twirls around to show you all sides of her new "do," and asks, "What do you think?" Does being honest mean you've got to say, "From my vantage point, dear, you look absolutely ridiculous!"

Speaking the truth in love doesn't mean being dishonest, but neither does it mean being brutally and cruelly honest. With honest words and a caring heart the wise husband could say, "Honey, I've got to hand it to you. You've always been creatively stylish, and this new hairdo fits you perfectly. I love that about you!"

Speaking the truth in love will allow you to overlook your own tastes and preferences. You can even love something you don't prefer because your loved one loves it—even a hairstyle you personally find ridiculous. The point is, honestly speaking the truth in love is about being considerate of another person's feelings.

As with acquiring a foreign language, learning the art of communication takes time, dedication, focus, and practice. Some of us may learn faster than others, so patience with your loved one is required. But like in any other art, learning to master it is a lifelong process.

8

COMMITMENT #6

I Choose to Love You by Demonstrating an Accepting, Loyal, and Enduring Love

Deep within at the core of your very being is the desire to be loved by another. God created you with that longing. You are a relational being with a legitimate need to be loved.

As a person who wants to be loved, try your hand at answering these three questions:

1. *What do you want to be loved for?* Think about it. Do you want to be loved for your looks? How about for your possessions or bank account? Do you want to be loved for your ability and skill in sports? For your musical talents? For your intellect? For the people you know and the influence you possess? Are these the reasons you want to be loved?

2. *How exclusively do you want to be loved?* Ponder that for a moment. Would you be satisfied to be among the top ten in your lover's life? You would be loved, but you would be only one of ten. Just how exclusively do you want to be loved?

3. *For how long do you want to be loved?* Pause and consider

how many years you want to be loved. Do you want to
be loved for five years, ten years, maybe twenty-five?
They say all good things must come to an end. Are you
comfortable setting a timeframe on how long you desire
to be loved?

I suspect you want to be loved, not for what you have or what
you can do, but for who you are. You want an *accepting love*.

I would guess you also want to be number one in someone's life.
You probably want someone to love you with all his or her heart and
love only you—exclusively you. You want a *loyal love*.

And finally, I would imagine you want a love that will last a lifetime. I imagine you're not comfortable agreeing to be loved during
the term of a three-year contract, for example. You want an *enduring love*.

I can assure you that your spouse also wants an accepting, loyal,
and enduring love. Whether you realize it or not, that is the kind
of love you committed to or will commit to in your marriage ceremony. This is the typical vow that is made in a wedding ceremony:

> I, (your name), take you, (spouse's name), to be my wed-
> ded husband/wife: to have and to hold, from this day
> forward, for better, for worse, for richer, for poorer, in
> sickness or in health, to love and to cherish, till death do
> us part. And hereto I pledge you my faithfulness.

What that vow says is that you both will have an accepting love
now and in the future. You are saying, "I love you for who you
are and will continue to love you unconditionally." As one pastor
observed, "In the vow there is no 'if.' Only 'and.'"

Your marriage vow is also stating that your love is going to be
loyal. You are saying, "I will make you my exclusive lover. You will
be my number one, with no one else in the picture, ever."

Your marriage vow is also one of permanency—an enduring love.

You are saying, "I will always love you and be there for you no matter what, until death parts us."

A love that is accepting, loyal, and enduring produces an intimate love relationship. It also engenders trust. Without trust, fear enters to create suspicion and doubts that in turn produce distance, coolness, and aloneness. Choose to love your spouse by demonstrating an accepting, loyal, and enduring love, and your relationship will deepen and grow.

Demonstrate an Accepting Love

Some of the most insecure relationships are experienced by couples who are always trying to live up to each other's expectations by their performance. We call this "performance-based acceptance." That kind of acceptance is often a carryover from childhood. When did your spouse feel most loved by his or her parents? Was it when mostly A's showed up on the report card? When his or her team won the game? When a task was completed just right? If your spouse was consistently rewarded based on what he or she did, then your spouse most likely equates love with doing all the right things—proper performance. If he or she performed right, love was felt. If he or she failed to perform up to expectation, the result was probably a sense of rejection.

For many of us this performance-based acceptance is programmed deep within us. We must in a real sense be deprogrammed from it into a "love you, period" acceptance. When you love your spouse with a "love, period" acceptance you are deepening a secure and trusting relationship that nurtures intimacy.

Think about the insecurity that persists in people who believe love has to be earned. They consciously or subconsciously fear they won't do this right or won't stop doing that wrong or can't fulfill this expectation or that one. It becomes a never-ending and exhausting treadmill of performance. But how freeing it is when they sense they are loved for who they are, period— regardless of their failings and shortcomings.

Imagine the security of knowing that you and your spouse will continue to love each other no matter what. Your husband forgets repeatedly to pick up his clothes as he said he would, but he still feels your love. Your wife seems to give more attention to her pet dog than she does to you at times, but you still love her. Your spouse's failings, shortcomings, weaknesses, flaws, and even downright misbehavior can and will be frustrating, but performance is not the basis of your love for him or her. Your love, an accepting love, is based on your commitment to that person, not on his or her performance.

Yet most people can't seem to get past their screw-ups and the paralyzing fear that love will be withheld if the performance isn't right. Your spouse may subconsciously think like that. Somehow poor performance becomes a major obstacle to feeling loved and accepted, period. On the other hand, you may wonder: *Will my acceptance only encourage continued misbehavior?* This kind of thinking is certainly an obstacle to giving unconditional acceptance in the first place. Unless you overcome this obstacle, your spouse will struggle to feel accepted without some kind of performance or condition. So how do you help your spouse feel accepted unconditionally?

Scripture tells us to "accept each other just as Christ has accepted you" (Romans 5:7). You can be sure if you accept your spouse as Christ accepts you, it will be the right kind of acceptance. But how does Jesus accept us? Does he accept us in spite of our performance? Scripture gives us many examples of Jesus' acceptance without preconditions. One of the most profound examples is Jesus' encounter with the Samaritan woman at the well. Reflecting upon the story gives us a vivid picture of what this acceptance looks like and how it produces security in a relationship. Let's unpack that story.

The Bible says Jesus "left Judea to return to Galilee. He had to go through Samaria on the way" (John 4:3-4). Jesus' travel itinerary is the first indicator of how accepting he is.

In fact, Jesus didn't have to go through Samaria to get to Galilee. The devoted Jews of the day would never go through Samaria to get to Galilee from Judea, though Galilee was due north of Judea and Samaria was right in the middle. Yet a Jewish person would either travel around that region by going east to Jericho and then following the Jordan Valley north, or might travel by boat west of the area via the Mediterranean Sea. A strict Jewish person would consider the longer journey well worth it.

Samaria had a long history of tension with Judea. In Jesus' day Jews considered Samaritans "half-breeds." They didn't believe they had the right pedigree (pure bloodline), so they wanted nothing to do with them. Additionally, Samaritans claimed that Mount Gerizim was the proper place to worship, while the Jews insisted that authentic worship could take place only in Jerusalem. In effect, Jews considered Samaritans heretics. So a "true follower" of Judaism would not dignify the Samaritans—or risk pollution—by even walking on their soil.

Jesus, being a Jew, should have had the same trouble with the tainted and "dysfunctional" background of the Samaritans. Your spouse may have carried his or her dysfunctional childhood background into your marriage. It sure would be a lot easier and less frustrating if you could walk around that dysfunction, wouldn't it? With all the mommy issues and daddy issues to put up with, it can really be troublesome. But an accepting love knows how to cope with the dysfunction, and Jesus demonstrated it. His accepting love walked right into the dysfunction without approving of it. We observe Jesus making his journey right through the middle of Samaria until he came to Sychar: "And Jesus, tired from the long walk, sat wearily beside the well [Jacob's well] about noontime" (John 4:6).

This was an arid and dry land. Water was a precious commodity. People would come to this well in the morning before the day heated up or in the cool of the evening. Few would come at noontime. Anyone drawing water at this time of day probably was trying to avoid being seen by the townspeople.

As Jesus sat near the well, he was alone, waiting for his disciples, who had gone into town to buy food. Then along came a Samaritan woman to draw water from the well. Not expecting to see anyone, she may have paid no attention to Jesus. Startled by the voice behind her she hears him say, "Please give me a drink" (verse 7).

The woman's response is significant: "You are a Jew, and I am a Samaritan woman. Why are you asking me for a drink?" (verse 9). This woman was shocked on two levels. First, this was a *man* who was talking to her. It was highly unusual for a man to speak to an unfamiliar woman. To do so was considered shameful, illicit, and at times even scandalous. Notice in verse 27 that when the disciples showed up, "They were astonished to find him talking to a woman." In that day men with good intentions just didn't talk to women who were strangers.

Secondly, Jewish men or women simply didn't converse with the heretical Samaritans. So it's clear the woman was taken aback by the very fact that he spoke to her. She must have thought, *This is a different kind of man.* Then notice what Jesus says: "If you only knew the gift God has for you and who I am, you would ask me, and I would give you living water" (verse 10).

Okay, it's one thing to accommodate the Samaritans' dysfunction by walking on their land, but offer this woman a gift? This will do nothing but incite more dysfunction, right? Tolerating your spouse's dysfunction is one thing, but encouraging it with "gift giving" is another. That kind of acceptance seems like too much. Yet that is precisely what Jesus did.

Jesus had this woman puzzled and interested. Not only did this man consider her worth talking to, he offered her an extraordinary gift. She knew the difference between "dead" and "living" water. "Living water" referred to moving water, like a fresh river or spring. "Dead water" was standing or stored water. This region of Samaria was far from any rivers, so Jesus' statement felt confusing. If Jacob had had to dig a well there, how could this man be offering her fresh, superior water?

But of course, if he could deliver on the fresh water idea, she was up for it. "Please sir," the woman said. "Give me some of that water! Then I'll never be thirsty again, and I won't have to come here to haul water" (verse 15).

Then Jesus threw her a big curve by saying, "Go and get your husband" (verse 16). Of course he knew she had had five previous husbands, and the man she was now living with wasn't her husband—and he told her that. Recognizing his prophetic power, she switched the subject to who was worshipping correctly, Jews or Samaritans.

Something must have begun to dawn on her. This man was truly different. He had spoken to a strange woman, which was unusual. He was Jewish and spoke to a Samaritan, which was even more unusual. Then he offered to direct her to some unknown fresh water source. And that was truly extraordinary. On top of all of that, he knew more about her than probably a lot of her neighbors. This led her to inquire about spiritual things like worship and the Messiah.

So she stated her own belief: "I know the Messiah will come— the one who is called Christ. When he comes, he will explain everything to us." Then Jesus revealed the truth of his relationship to her: "I am the Messiah!" (verses 25-26). He was saying, in effect, "Yes, I may be a man, and I may be a Jewish man, but I'm really your Messiah, your deliverer, the one you have been longing for." At that point in her excitement, she headed back to the village to spread the news of whom she had met.

This Samaritan woman had never encountered such a man— one who was so receptive, so open to her, so welcoming. She knew Jesus had no reason to accept her as he did. She must have felt alienated, rejected, and alone. But despite all that, this extraordinary Jesus received her.

Think about your relationship with your spouse. Let's say he or she is far from perfect, with a lot of baggage from childhood or from another marital relationship that went bad. Let's even say your spouse hasn't been on his or her best behavior lately. What would Jesus say to your spouse? Despite all the dysfunction he would say, "I am your deliverer, the one you have been longing for. I know what you've gone through, and even though I am aware of all your 'stuff,' I look beyond that and love you for being you." If your love had that much acceptance, how do you think your spouse would feel? Don't you think he or she would feel deeply secure in that kind of love?

That is what a Christlike acceptance does—it looks beyond your faults and loves the real you. Interestingly, Jesus' extraordinary acceptance without condition doesn't condone the faults and wrong in a person's life. He didn't approve of the woman's adultery. Yet he still saw the beauty, the potential, the innate worth, and the dignity that God had invested in her and in every human by virtue of their creation in his image, and he loved her for that. Nor was he "judging her" for not worshipping correctly. He was the compassionate corrector, loving her enough to tell her the truth. Jesus' acceptance of her had nothing to do with her own actions. Nothing she could say or do (or not say or not do) would cause the Messiah to show her such respect and let her know she was welcome in his presence. He accepted her as she was and gave her a vision of who she could become. That is the nature and love of our God, who accepts on the basis of his character, not our performance.

So how does he do that? And how can we show such an accepting love to our spouse? The key is in the nature of the relationship and in separating what a person does from who that person is.

When Jesus accepted the Samaritan woman he didn't just overlook her sin and in effect say, "That's okay, everybody messes up. I'll just forget your past sins." God's absolute holiness keeps him from doing that. He can't just overlook sin. The Bible says of him, "Your eyes are too pure to look on evil; you cannot tolerate wrongdoing" (Habakkuk 1:13 NIV). He is so holy that he "cannot allow sin in any form" (Habakkuk 1:13 NLT). So what does he do?

God makes a distinction between your "essence," created in his image, and your "nature," infected because of sin. The Bible says that "your iniquities have separated you from your God" (Isaiah 59:2 NIV). Isaiah makes a clear distinction between you as God's lost child, created in his image, and what you do—sin. Because what you do is *not* the same as who you are. If that were the case, God couldn't remove "our sin as far from us as the east is from the west" (Psalm 103:12).

In effect God is saying, "You are my child, created in my image. That is who you are. Your misbehavior is wrong. I can't overlook that. In fact I hate what it has done to you—it has separated you from me. So I will sacrifice my only Son and allow him to endure a cruel death on the cross to satisfy my perfect justice. This is how much we both love you. And if you will accept my Son's death as yours, I will remove the curse of sin from you, and you will no longer be my lost child, but my found child."

Following God's example, you can accept your spouse in a similar way. He is your loving husband. She is your devoted wife. That is the relationship you enjoy. Face it, his behavior or her actions do not always reflect a pure devotion and perfect love to you. But don't assign the misbehavior, faults, and failures to him or her as your committed husband or wife. See the faults and weaknesses separately from that committed relationship. Forgive and separate them from the person; then accept him or her as the loving husband or wife you married.

This really works best when both of you are doing your best to love each other. Dottie can testify that I really mess up at times. I'm not as considerate as I should be, I say things that are cutting, and I hurt her when I get angry, I don't show her my appreciation as much as I should—I could go on and on. But does she consider me a despicable husband? Not at all. Why? Because of two things. One, she accepts me for who I am, where I am. And secondly, I seek her forgiveness when I mess up. Dottie separates my specific mistakes of behavior from the true person I am and accepts me without condition. That motivates me to apologize to her when I blow it. She says, "I can't always put my trust in Josh's performance, because he's not perfect. But I can always trust his heart. His performance at times may be faulty, but his intentions are pure."

Dottie and I accept each other for who we are. That convinces both of us that we don't need to earn love by performing right, while at the same time it highly motivates us to make the security, welfare, and happiness of the other as important as our own. In the process we build a strong trust, confidence that both of us deeply want to please the other.

Love your spouse with an accepting love! Keep loving that way, and you too will enjoy a secure and intimate relationship.

Demonstrate a Loyal Love

"Laura, honey, how was your vacation?" Jim says as he embraces Laura with a body-to-body hug. Megan, Jim's wife, looks on uneasily as he invites Laura to sit down and give details about her trip to the Bahamas.

Megan sits down with the two as Laura recounts some of the sights she visited. Jim looks intently into Laura's eyes as she speaks, touching her hand, and patting her shoulder occasionally as he responds to her stories. Megan has endured Jim's forward behavior with women during their two years of marriage, but she has never liked it. Jim claims he's just being friendly. Megan feels he's flirty. They often get into arguments about it.

She also says Jim was that demonstrative toward her when they were dating. He focused entirely on her then, seeming to ignore other women. But since they have been married, he no longer looks intently into her eyes and does not "touch" her as he does other women. Megan admits she is jealous and doesn't feel she is wrong in feeling that way.

Is Megan wrong to be jealous of the way Jim acts toward other women? The Bible condemns jealousy. It says, "You are still controlled by your sinful nature. You are jealous of one another and quarrel with each other" (1 Corinthians 3:3). Isn't Megan being uptight and possessive? Shouldn't she lighten up and give her husband freedom to admire other women?

Imagine me being on my honeymoon with Dottie. We are strolling romantically along a beach. I turn to her, look deeply into her eyes, and say, "Dottie, honey, of all the more than three billion women on this planet, you are on my top-10 list." You watch as my new wife leans her head on my shoulder and gazes into my eyes. "Gee, Josh, thanks. That means so much. It thrills me to think that I'm among the ten women you love! Just to be on your list, sweetheart, is good enough for me."

Can you imagine that kind of response? I can't. Dottie would be insulted, hurt, and upset if I romantically loved even one other woman besides her. And she should be. My wife wants to be number one in my life. And I want to be considered the number-one man in her life. You and I were relationally created that way. We are designed to jealously want each other's exclusive love.

That kind of jealousy isn't wrong, and neither is Megan's. God himself exhibits jealousy, and that is far from being wrong. In Exodus it says, "You must worship no other gods, for the LORD, whose very name is Jealous, is a God who is jealous about his relationship with you" (Exodus 34:14). Joshua also told the children of Israel that their God was "a holy and jealous God" (Joshua 24:19). These two words "jealous God" in the Hebrew are *el qana,* which denotes passion and zeal. Although the word *jealous* in English is mostly used in a negative sense, in the Hebrew it expresses passion and caring, most often in connection with the marriage relationship. God described the children of Israel using the image of being married to them, and he wanted them to love him as a wife would devote herself exclusively to her husband. He said they were to worship no other God but him. He wants to be loved with a pure and faithful love, a love reserved only for him. In fact, his jealous or loyal love is a model for us to follow.

When you reserve your love and devotion exclusively for your spouse it deepens the relationship. An exclusive or loyal love is expressed in at least two ways. A loyal love is *pure* and a loyal love is *faithful*.

Loyalty means being pure. Scripture says, "Marriage should be honored by all, and the marriage bed kept pure" (Hebrews 13:4 NIV). We are to maintain a pure marital relationship, but what does it mean exactly to be pure?

Have you ever had a candy bar that identified itself on the wrapper as "pure milk chocolate"? What about a jar of honey? Some labels read "Pure honey—no artificial sweeteners." Purity of chocolate or honey means there is no foreign substance to contaminate it or to keep it from being or tasting what authentic chocolate or pure honey is supposed to be and taste like.

To keep the marriage bed pure means a husband and wife are to keep their emotional and physical relations exclusively between them. To have more than one sexual partner would be to bring a foreign substance into the relationship, and it would cease to be pure. If you were to drop a dirty pebble into a glass of pure water, it would become adulterated—or impure. A glass of water without any impurities in it is unadulterated. A pure, unadulterated sex life leads to an intimate, secure relationship.

I believe God designed sex to be experienced within an unbroken circle, a pure union between two virgins entering into an exclusive relationship. That pure union can be broken even *before* marriage, if one or both of the partners has not kept the marriage bed pure by waiting to have sex within the purity of a husband-wife relationship. Remaining pure until marriage doubly reinforces the trust factor between them. That doesn't mean couples who have not waited to have sex until marriage can't build a trusting relationship in marriage. But virginity at marriage shows a commitment to purity and promotes trust.

Before I was married I dated a young lady named Paula. We dated for three and a half years and almost got married. Even though we were very compatible and enjoyed and respected each other immensely, we didn't feel we were right for each other as a married couple. We finally broke up but continued to be friends.

Three years later I met Dottie. Soon after we were married, Dottie met Paula. They became good friends and started spending a lot of time together. Eventually, Paula moved close to our home in California. We practically became neighbors.

One morning I arrived home from a trip, and Dottie wasn't there. When she returned she told me she had spent the morning with Paula. She came over, put her arms around me, and said, "Honey, I'm sure glad you behaved yourself for three and a half years."

I took a deep breath and asked hesitantly, "Why?"

Dottie responded, "Paula shared with me this morning that she was so in love with you that there were times she would have done anything for you, but you never once took advantage of her." Needless to say, I sighed with relief, and I was profoundly glad I had never pushed Paula in the area of the physical.

Do you know what that said to my wife? It reinforced her confidence: *I can trust my husband!* Not everyone can say they have kept their single life pure sexually. But if you can, it sends a doubly strong signal to your spouse that you are worthy of trust. If you can stay pure before you're married, it strengthens you to stay true afterward.

Marriage is to be pure: unadulterated, without any extramarital affairs. When a man guards himself against flirtation and establishes healthy boundaries with women, it builds trust and deepens the relationship. The same is true with a wife. When she is careful with how she dresses and how she carries herself around other men, it builds trust and deepens the relationship. A loyal love seeks to keep any and all foreign elements from adulterating the relationship.

Loyalty means being faithful. A loyal love is also faithful. "To have and to hold" the wedding vow says, "for better, for worse, for richer, for poorer, in sickness and in health…hereto I pledge you my faithfulness." Being faithful means keeping your promise not only to be exclusive sexually with your spouse, but to be there emotionally for him or her too.

Megan felt jealous because Jim was giving his affection to someone other than her. No, he did not have sex with other women, but he was still wrong in showing other women such affection. Faithfulness means more than being sexually faithful.

When the apostle Paul writes that we are to "avoid sexual immorality" (1 Thessalonians 4:3 NASB), he follows up with a powerful word to describe how a man should not take advantage of another man's wife. He says a man must not "defraud his brother in the matter" (1 Thessalonians 4:6). The word "defraud" means to rob or take away something that belongs to another.

Sexual relationships belong exclusively within marriage. If a man steps in and has sex with another man's wife he is taking what belongs solely between a husband and wife. He is defrauding—taking something from the other man that he has no right to take. In a marriage relationship on a broader level, when a married man gives intimate devotion and affection to another man's wife or wife-to-be, he is defrauding or robbing his own wife. The devotion and affection that belonged to Megan was being given to Laura. Megan had a right to feel jealous. Jim wasn't staying true to his vows to love and cherish and stay emotionally faithful to Megan exclusively. Her trust was undermined, and it negatively affected the relationship.

That's another thing about a loyal love that is pure and faithful: it protects the relationship from negative consequences. It also provides many benefits. Dottie and I were both virgins when we married, and we have stayed sexually faithful after marriage. That means we never had to go through the heartache of a pregnancy before marriage. Consequently, we have not experienced the heart-wrenching ordeal of relinquishing a child for adoption or struggling with getting married before we were ready because of pregnancy.

We have been protected from the fear that any sexually transmitted disease might come into our lives.

We have been protected from the sexual insecurity that can come from being compared to past lovers one's spouse may have had. And consequently, we have experienced trust in our relationship.

We have also been protected from the feelings of betrayal that an extramarital affair can cause. As a result we have enjoyed relational intimacy unobstructed by breaches of trust or ghosts from the past. That is what loyal love does. It is pure and faithful to the other person sexually and emotionally, and that produces trust.

Demonstrating an Enduring Love

You may be young and just starting out in a love relationship. Or you may be quite a few years into a married relationship. But count on it, if you avoid accidents and remain relatively healthy, something called age is going to catch up to you.

When your skin goes all wrinkly and your hair turns gray, what will your wife think of you then? What will you think when that happens to her? When your fat cells multiply and your body bulges out here, there, and everywhere, what will she feel about you then? How will you feel if the same happens to her? What happens if one of you can't keep up with the other's energy? How will you feel then? As you age, one or both of you may begin to suffer the loss of eyesight, hearing, or mobility. Your physical attractiveness may fade and your sexual desire diminish, and you both become less than what you once were. How will you both feel toward each other then?

When you think of the future, do you fear he won't be attracted to you any longer? Do you fear she'll miss the man that once was and worry that the love flame that once burned bright will somehow become dim? How can you be sure the love you do have will last—considering the alluring attractiveness of others who are prettier than you, smarter than you, richer than you, better-built than you, funnier than you and, overall, more appealing than you are? Can your spouse be sure that though you said, "Till death do us part," you will still be there when age has ravaged his or her body? The confidence you will stand by your spouse—no matter what—comes from your enduring love. Your spouse needs the assurance that your love will continue forever. That assurance flows from a committed love that won't give up and won't let him or her down.

That kind of love is modeled by God, whose "faithful love endures forever" (Psalm 136:1). "The LORD always keeps his promises; he is gracious in all he does" (Psalm 145:13). "Your eternal word, O LORD, stands firm in heaven. Your faithfulness extends to every generation" (Psalm 119:89-90). "He will never fail you nor abandon you" (Deuteronomy 31:6), "for he loves us with unfailing love; the LORD's faithfulness endures forever" (Psalm 117:2). "Trust your lives to the God who created you, for he will never fail you" (1 Peter 4:19). And in Jesus' own words, "Be sure of this: I am with you always, even to the end of the age" (Matthew 28:20).

How can you be sure your love for each other will stay strong—no matter what—and last a lifetime? Humans falter and fail—they are not perfect like God. Yet I believe an enduring love can be empowered by him if we place our trust in him to enable us to love our spouse and nurture that love daily. I have watched couples go through difficulty and seen how they let their love die. I have also watched couples go through difficulty and seen how their commitment to one another simply refuses to let the relationship grow cold. You can choose to make your love the kind that lasts.

An enduring love that says, "I'll be there for you" isn't a fairy tale. It's real. You can allow the never-ending, never-failing love of God to empower your own love for your spouse and keep it fresh and vibrant. Go back to the first commitment: "I choose to love you by making God a priority in my life." God designed marriage as a three-way proposition. He loves your spouse with a faithful love that endures forever. Do you think it would please him to channel some of that enduring love through you? He certainly is willing and able. And as you keep clear channels open to him, he can empower you to love your mate with love that will last. As you do it he will fuel your enduring love. "Love never gives up, never loses faith, is always hopeful, and endures through every circumstance" (1 Corinthians 13:7).

Difficulties and struggles are a part of life and marriage. Your love for your spouse needs to be accepting, loyal, and enduring in order to overcome those difficulties and struggles. But no matter what you do or how much you love your spouse, conflicts will arise. The issue isn't to try to avoid conflicts as much as it is to know how to resolve conflicts. That is the subject of the next chapter.

9

COMMITMENT #7

I Choose to Love You by
Resolving Conflicts Quickly

He couldn't keep his anger bottled up, and Jennifer caught the brunt of it. Oliver loved Jennifer and realized he had hurt her, so he started to apologize. Jennifer cut him off by saying, "Love means never having to say you're sorry."

That well-known line comes from the 1970 film *Love Story*. It has been quoted and ridiculed by tens of thousands ever since. It appears that if you could be in a love relationship in which you never had to say you're sorry, you would be free of conflict. But that would mean either that you were perfect or were living with a robot with no feelings. If you're living in the real world, you are going to encounter conflicts with the person you love. And admitting you're wrong is a part of conflict resolution.

The very fact that people are different from each other makes conflict inevitable. We bring different backgrounds, viewpoints, emotions, and even different cultures into our relationships. It is natural that these differences will cause conflicts. Being of two different sexes always provides potential for conflict. As one marriage counselor put it, "There are two things that cause unhappy marriages—men and women!"

We subconsciously develop certain expectations about the person we date or marry. It's not realistic that all those expectations can be met, and when they're not, we're disappointed and even find ourselves in conflict. It would be great if the ideal wife or husband existed, but often what we would like in a spouse and what we get are worlds apart.

Differences, unrealized expectations, and the very fact that we are human means there will be conflicts sooner or later. *Having* conflict, then, is not the issue. The real test is whether we can *resolve* conflicts—and quickly, before they disrupt the relationship.

Choosing to love by resolving conflicts quickly can be done, in part, by believing in and committing to the principle that *it is more rewarding to resolve a conflict than to dissolve the relationship*. This means embracing commitment as a foundational principle of marriage. Over 1000 people were asked in a survey, "Why do you think divorce is so common today?" Respondents were divided into those aged 18 to 49 and those 50-plus. Interestingly, there was a consensus between these two age groups: 43 percent of those ages 50 and above and 47 percent of those under 50 said, "Marriage isn't taken as seriously as it used to be."[1]

Committing to the marriage relationship for the long haul is essential and requires conflict resolution. As a couple, you should agree that dissolving the relationship isn't really an option for you. If you have children, give them a gift of security—let them know you are committed to stay together as a married couple.

One day when Sean was six years old, I noticed he wasn't quite himself when he came home from school. I asked what was wrong.

"Aw, nothing, Dad," he said.

Sean and I enjoyed pretty good communication so I said, "Come on, share with me what you're feeling."

He hesitated, and then he asked, "Daddy, are you going to leave Mommy?"

I knew that question would come up someday. "What makes you ask that?" I inquired.

Sean told me that three of his friends' dads had just divorced their mothers, and he was afraid I might do the same.

I sat down with Sean, looked him in the eye, and said, "I want you to know one thing. I love your mother very much. I'm committed to her, and I'll never leave her. Period."

That little six-year-old breathed a sigh of relief, smiled at me, and said, "Thanks, Dad." At that moment he didn't need reinforcement of my love for him so much as he needed the security that comes from knowing that his mother and I love each other and are committed to a permanent relationship. He knew, like the rest of our children, that Dad and Mom disagreed about things, and sometimes the kids even saw Dottie and me arguing. That wasn't all bad as long as they also saw how we resolved the conflicts.

Let your kids know that though you and your spouse at times disagree with each other, it doesn't mean you love each other any less. It doesn't signal you might get a divorce. Assure them you are always committed to resolve the conflict rather than dissolve the relationship.

Unhealthy Responses to Conflict

Sometimes our natural tendencies in dealing with conflicts can be negative and unhealthy. I don't know of anyone who truly enjoys relational conflict. And instead of responding positively to conflict resolution, many of us react negatively, mostly because we fear it's going to hurt. It seems no matter how you try, you are bound to get hurt somewhere along the way in resolving conflicts—and it's no fun getting hurt. But being vulnerable and exposing yourself to someone who loves you is part of the process.

There are millions of people who go through life constantly trying to insulate themselves from relational and emotional pain. They crave and search for real emotional intimacy, but they can never find it in their relationships because they can't bring themselves to open up and be vulnerable. We must resist the natural tendency to protect ourselves and instead be willing to be vulnerable if we are going to resolve relational conflicts.

It's natural to protect what we care about. But when that protective behavior becomes selfish it produces unhealthy responses that make it harder to resolve conflicts. Consider ten ineffective or unhealthy responses that many people try to use to resolve conflicts:

1. *Problem? What problem?* Ignore a problem long enough…will it go away? Not likely. Deny there is a conflict, and the conflict remains unresolved.

2. *The silent treatment.* We know there is a problem but we don't talk about it. We just hide out by refusing to bring the problem into the open and deal with it.

3. *It's no big deal.* Ignoring the significance of the conflict doesn't make it go away either. Instead it can grow into a much larger problem.

4. *Well, all things work together for good.* Overspiritualizing the problem sometimes means we're not sincere about resolving it.

5. *Keeping score.* When we bottle up conflicts, anger, and resentment and keep a tally of how they grow, sooner or later somebody will explode.

6. *Attacking the person instead of the problem.* People are to be loved and problems are to be solved; it's not the other way around.

7. *It's your fault.* Blaming usually means that the person pointing the finger is unable to admit his or her own failures.

8. *I'm right—you're wrong.* The desire to win at all costs will not resolve anything. Someone will go away full of resentment.

9. *I surrender.* Giving in just to avoid conflict only keeps the pain alive. Neither one goes away feeling that anything was accomplished.

10. *Bribery.* Instead of dealing with a conflict, some people try to buy their way out of the situation by offering a special gift.

Resolving Relational Conflicts

You may have recognized yourself in one or more of the above unhealthy responses to conflict. Many of us have not been taught how to resolve relationship conflicts. There have been volumes written on the subject that can be very helpful. I encourage you to check out the many Christian books on conflict resolution. Let me share with you five principles that have guided Dottie and me in resolving conflicts in our own marriage.

Keep a clean slate. It was a hectic morning. I had a number of important meetings, and I was running late. During breakfast Dottie brought a folder full of her agenda items to add to my already filled day. I was trying to deflect each one with a passive response like "Okay," "I'll get to that," "Yes, that sounds good," and "All right, I'll try." But Dottie could sense I wasn't really listening and had little intention of getting to her to-do list any time soon. She bored in and attempted to nail me down.

I lost it. In front of the kids I started arguing with her. Finally I exploded. I threw her folder down on the table and said, "I'm out of here." I stormed out the door and drove off.

I didn't get a mile down the road until I said to myself, *McDowell, what in the world is up with you? Get yourself back to the house and clear the slate with your wife.* I turned around, went back to the house, and asked all the kids to join me in the kitchen along with Dottie. I apologized to her for blowing up and asked her to forgive me for hurting her. I turned to the kids and told them I was wrong for being so disrespectful to their mother and asked them to forgive me too. I then asked Dottie if we could have some time alone to bring closure to our conflict.

I quoted this verse before but it bears repeating. "Don't sin by letting anger control you. Don't let the sun go down while you are still angry" (Ephesians 4:6). I was guilty of the first sentence of that verse. I let my anger control me, and I exploded. But I wasn't going to be guilty of the second part of that verse. Before the day went by, I was determined to wipe the slate clean by asking Dottie to forgive me.

There is no serious relationship problem that didn't begin with a series of small conflicts that were left unresolved. A marital affair, emotional abuse, pornography addiction—you name it—all major problems are preceded by little unresolved issues here or there. Quickly take care of these little things as they come up. Clean the slate and keep the slate clean. That is an important principle in resolving relational conflicts.

Acknowledge your fallibility. You and I know that we are not perfect. Everybody blows it—and we know that. Yet our emotions resist admitting it. Sure, it hurts to be wrong. It's a hard thing to acknowledge that we failed somehow. But acknowledging, accepting, and embracing our fallibility is a prerequisite to resolving conflicts.

It is rare indeed that a conflict with the one you love is one-sided. In the vast majority of cases both people bear some responsibility. Admitting you're wrong isn't saying you're a bad person; it's saying you're a normal person. Your spouse or loved one knows your heart and realizes you have good intentions even though you don't always carry out what you plan or even want to do. The apostle Paul understood this clearly: "The Spirit gives us desires that are opposite from what the sinful nature desires. These two forces are constantly fighting each other, and your choices are never free from this conflict" (Galatians 5:17-18 NLT).

It is humbling to admit you are wrong and accept criticism from someone, even the one who loves you the most. But it is worth it. Solomon wisely said, "If you ignore criticism, you will end in poverty and disgrace; if you accept correction, you will be honored" (Proverbs 13:18). So when you are wrong, admit it. When you are right, keep quiet. That is a sound policy for resolving conflict.

The apostle Paul tells us that "God, who began a good work within you, will continue his work until it is finally finished" (Philippians 1:6). No mistake is fatal. Someone has said, "God is greater than the greatest goofs." All of us are in process, and it is a sign of health to admit your failings. Your spouse probably had a clue somewhere along the line that you were not perfect when he or she married you. And I'd say he or she is willing to give you a second, third, fourth, fifth, and many, many more chances to do it right. The key is to accept your fallibility. That doesn't mean to wear it as a badge of honor or use it as an excuse for irresponsible behavior. It means to admit your failings without believing you're a failure and to accept your wrongs by seeking forgiveness. Again, Solomon tells us, "A man [or a woman] who refuses to admit his mistakes can never be successful. But if he confesses and forsakes them, he gets another chance" (Proverbs 28:13 TLB).

Take responsibility for your negative emotional reactions. Acknowledging you are fallible is important. It is humbling to admit you are not perfect. As I said, it is natural to be defensive when we blow it or when we are accused of something. But if we are going to resolve conflicts in a relationship we must take responsibility for our negative emotional reactions by bringing them into the light and confessing them.

Admitting I'm wrong is not easy. When I was driving down the road after blowing my top with Dottie, I knew inside I was wrong. I could have shrugged and said to myself, *Okay, you shouldn't have reacted that way. Do better next time.* I could have driven on to my appointments and just forgotten about it. But inwardly admitting

I was wrong wasn't enough to resolve the conflict. I had hurt Dottie, and I had to take the next step by confessing to her I was wrong and seeking her forgiveness. (We'll cover the importance of forgiveness in detail in the next chapter.)

I could have also given myself a pass by thinking, *Dottie was wrong for pressing me like that. She knows how busy I am. So if I apologize, it will tell her she can keep on pressuring me, and I certainly don't want that.*

Taking responsibility for your own negative reactions to something your spouse did or said isn't in any way condoning his or her behavior. Your spouse may have been completely wrong in what he or she did, yet that doesn't justify a negative reaction. You may be prone to say, "Well, the reason I reacted that way is because you…" and then go on to explain how his or her words or actions caused your negative emotional reaction.

The truth is, in most cases people don't really cause us to react negatively: we choose how to respond—in explosion or silence. More often than not, their actions simply reveal that we were under stress, with an inner powder keg of emotional explosives connected to a short fuse about to go off. We need to learn to disconnect that fuse before someone else unknowingly sparks it. And of course we need to deal with the pent-up emotions that can lead to a verbal bomb. We must own up to it—we are responsible for our own emotional reactions.

Did you ever notice that what bothers you the most about someone is often something that is true of you? It really bugged me that Dottie was needling me about getting this and that done "today." You know that urgency in the voice that says, "I need this right away. Can you have it done this morning?" Yet that is precisely what I do to other people. I get all anxious about needing something sent to me by 9:00 a.m., and I put the pressure on my assistant. And once it arrives I may not get to it for two or three days. I find it annoying when someone does that to me, but I am perfectly comfortable doing it to others.

Jesus talked about people like me when he said,

> Why worry about a speck in your friend's eye when you have a log in your own? How can you think of saying to your friend, "Let me help you get rid of that speck in your eye" when you can't see past the log in your own eye? Hypocrite! First get rid of the log in your own eye; then you will see well enough to deal with the speck in your friend's eye (Matthew 7:3-5).

Am I the only one with that problem? I doubt it. We all need to follow Jesus' teaching and example and take responsibility for our own negative emotional reactions. That is a necessary step in resolving our relational conflicts.

See from the other person's point of view. Most, if not all, misunderstandings are a result of differing assumptions. A husband sees something from his vantage point, while the wife sees it from hers—and neither one of them is aware of their differing assumptions. That is so common.

When my hair started thinning a little I thought I'd start using aerosol hairspray. One morning Dottie and I were both standing at the sink, and I pulled out my hairspray. As soon as I started using it Dottie said, "Honey, please don't do that."

Being the considerate husband I am, I stepped back from the sink and proceeded to use my spray. She looked over at me and said, "What are you doing? I told you that bothers me." I looked at her as if to say, *Who do you think you are?* I didn't say anything, but my actions spoke volumes. I tossed the can of spray toward the counter, and it broke a bottle of Dottie's favorite cologne—expensive cologne. Then I stormed out of the house.

Dottie couldn't figure out why I reacted so negatively. I couldn't figure out what she had against me spraying my hair. The problem was that both of us failed to see from the other's point of view. We were ignorant of our differing assumptions.

In all my years around my wife I had never become aware of her disdain for aerosol cans. She hated spray cans. She believed they contributed to our pollution (and she was right). She had forbidden the kids to use them, but I was in the dark on how she felt about hairspray.

I hadn't shared with Dottie how I was a little concerned about my hair thinning and how I thought hairspray might help. She didn't understand where I was coming from any more than I understood her position. That set up a perfect condition for conflict.

It didn't take us long to resolve our conflict once we sat down to understand each other's point of view. By the way, Dottie's view prevailed, and I didn't use aerosol cans of hairspray after that.

When you sense a conflict with your spouse or loved one is in the making, take a time out and seek to know his or her point of view. Say something like, "I don't want to upset you; nor do I want to get upset. Please help me to understand your point of view. Could you please explain where you're coming from?" The previous chapters on being a good listener and learning the art of communication are so important here. We are on the road to resolving conflicts when we seek to understand the other person's view more than to be understood ourselves.

Understand that resolving isn't the same as agreeing. Can a conservative Republican marry a liberal Democrat and have a happy marriage? Can a fanatical Washington Redskins fan be married to a devoted Dallas Cowboys fan and live together peaceably? Resolving relational conflicts doesn't mean you will agree with your spouse on everything. In fact sharp differences may provide needed balance in a couple's life.

Solomon wrote, "As iron sharpens iron, so a friend sharpens a friend" (Proverbs 27:17). Our differences can actually become strengths. God has assembled his body, the Church, with different members—like different parts of the body—for the purpose of unity and strength. He wants the differences between husband and wife to unify and strengthen their marriage. The apostle Paul points out how the differences of the hands and feet and eyes and ears fulfill different roles—yet all are needed. He concludes,

> In fact, some parts of the body that seem weakest and least important are actually the most necessary. And the parts we regard as less honorable are those we clothe with greatest care. So we carefully protect those parts that should not be seen, while the more honorable parts do not require this special care (1 Corinthians 12:22-24).

Your perspective and gifting is no doubt different from your spouse. These differences are not to be eliminated, but rather brought together to strengthen the marriage and create wholeness between the two of you. Your spouse is there, in part, to balance you out. The fact that he is wired differently from you and that she sees life and relationships differently from you is part of God's design: You need each other because your differences can complement and complete each other—in his service, with gifts united to help others. Being the same (agreeing on every issue and seeing from the same perspective) would be lopsided and incomplete.

My good friend and ministry consultant Bobb Biehl talks about this needed diversity as "maximizing each other's strengths and making our weaknesses irrelevant." Work to resolve your conflicts, but allow your differences to complement and complete you.

Be committed to resolve the conflicts rather than dissolve the relationship.

Keep the slate clean and be quick to

- address the conflict
- acknowledge your fallibility

- take responsibility for your negative emotional reactions
- see from the other person's point of view
- understand that resolving isn't the same as agreeing

Scripture provides good advice for resolving conflicts and living in unity: "Always be humble and gentle. Be patient with each other, making allowances for each other's faults because of your love. Make every effort to keep yourselves united in the Spirit, binding yourselves together with peace" (Ephesians 4:2-3).

Commitment #8

I Choose to Love You by Always Forgiving You

His shirt and pants showed no sign of wrinkles. You could almost see yourself in his highly polished shoes. He sat down beside me, and we struck up a conversation. I learned he was a highly paid consultant in corporate relational development and problem solving. When I asked what problem he encountered most, he immediately replied, "The inability to resolve personal conflicts in the workplace."

I inquired, "What's the number-one obstacle in overcoming personal conflicts?" Without batting an eye he responded, "Forgiveness." He said his greatest challenge was getting people to let go of their grudges and give and accept forgiveness.

Closeness in a love relationship and intimacy in a marriage are impossible without each of us giving and accepting forgiveness. Without this, lingering grudges and guilt will drive you crazy. In fact the director of a mental institution in Knoxville, Tennessee, once told me that 50 percent of the patients could go home if they only knew they were forgiven.

We live in a culture overrun with stored-up grudges, resentments, bitterness, and unforgiving hearts. We need forgiveness. It is forgiveness that oils a relationship. It reduces the friction and allows us to become close to others. If you believe a person is unforgiving, you will hesitate to reveal your vulnerabilities.

So much hinges on your ability to give and accept forgiveness, including everything we have covered so far. Think about it: making God a priority in your life, loving and accepting yourself for who you are, learning to be an other-focused lover, becoming a great listener, learning to communicate, demonstrating an accepting, loyal, and enduring love, and resolving conflicts quickly. All these are possible only if you can seek forgiveness, forgive others, and accept forgiveness for yourself.

What Is Forgiveness?

There are a number of ways to define forgiveness. Here are two:

1. *Forgiveness means* to erase, to forego what is due; to give up resentment; to wipe the slate clean, to release from a debt, to cancel punishment; to personally accept the price of reconciliation; to give up all claims on one who has hurt you and let go of the emotional consequences of that hurt. It means not only to say, "I forgive you," but also to give up the emotional consequences of the hurt. Forgiveness calls for action, which means it doesn't wait for someone to ask for it.

2. *Forgiveness also means* to give up or give away. If someone violates your rights, forgiveness means you give up the right of reaction and the right to get even, no matter how much you may feel revenge is justified. To forgive means to give mercy, not to demand justice.

We are commanded to forgive. Jesus said, "If you forgive those who sin against you, your heavenly Father will forgive you. But if you refuse to forgive others, your Father will not forgive your sins" (Matthew 6:15).

On first reading you might think Jesus is saying that our own forgiveness is based on our forgiveness of others. We know from other passages of Scripture that God's forgiveness of our sin is based solely on Christ and his atoning sacrificial death on our behalf. So then what does our forgiveness of others have to do with his forgiveness of us?

I believe Jesus is saying that those who are unwilling to forgive others have yet to truly experience God's mercy and grace. Because once a person understands the depth of what his or her sins have caused—the immeasurable suffering and death of the innocent and perfect Son of God—it naturally results in repentance, and that repentance unleashes the amazing grace—the unmerited favor—of God's mercy and love. How could those who have truly experienced such mercy not also give mercy to others? I believe that is what Jesus is saying.

Our model and standard for forgiving others is God's mercy and grace to us expressed in the loving and sacrificial death of Christ. We don't deserve his forgiveness—it is his unmerited favor toward us. We can't earn it—it is already "paid for you with the precious life-blood of Christ, the sinless, spotless Lamb of God" (1 Peter 1:19 NLT).

Even though we don't deserve it nor can we earn it, God's forgiveness is so complete that our offenses are forever blotted out and forgotten.

It is true that all of us deserve punishment for our sins, but Scripture tells us that God "does not punish us for all our sins; he does not deal harshly with us, as we deserve. For his unfailing love toward those who fear him is as great as the height of the heavens above the earth" (Psalm 103:10-11). Then the Bible goes on to say how far our sins are taken away from us. "He has removed our sins as far from us as the east is from the west" (Psalm 103:12).

Why does Scripture say "as far from us as the east is from the west" rather than "as far as the north is from the south?" From east to west is a Hebrew expression for infinity. You can measure the north from the south (there are a North Pole and a South Pole, but you cannot measure the distance from the east to the west. If you go east or if you travel west, you could go in that direction forever. It is like saying your sins have been obliterated. You could travel anywhere and never find a trace of them to condemn you before God. Think of it—"the LORD is compassionate and merciful, slow to get angry and filled with unfailing love" (Psalm 103:8), and your sins have vanished forever because his forgiveness is absolute. This is quite a model and standard by which to forgive others.

What Forgiveness Isn't

Forgiveness is not just saying, "Well, I'm sorry." When we do that, we are acknowledging the problem but not our responsibility for getting ourselves off the hook. Forgiveness is saying, "I was wrong. I'm sorry. Will you forgive me?" And it is also important to specifically state what it is we are seeking forgiveness for.

Forgiveness is not conditional. We can't really ensure that a person will change. Forgiveness isn't saying, "Maybe if you clean up your life, then I'll forgive you." Forgiveness isn't about negotiating with someone to behave differently.

Forgiveness is not pretending that the situation never happened. Some people just go on with life and act as though there never was a problem. If this is how a person deals with a situation, the problem will inevitably come back to haunt him or her.

Forgiveness is not indifference. If the attitude is "So what?" it indicates a person does not understand the gravity of the problem.

Forgiveness is not condoning wrong. Resolving the personal hurt through forgiveness doesn't mean that we condone a wrong action.

Forgiveness is not just saying, "Let's forget about it." The problem is that our emotions generally don't forget about it. In many cases the unresolved issue becomes a source of irritation or resentment. Forgetting does not result in forgiveness. It's really the other way around: quite often forgiveness can result in forgetting.

Forgiveness is not tolerance. Simply forever putting up with a problem doesn't resolve anything and cannot help a relationship.

Finally, forgiveness is not a feeling. At times we may feel like forgiving someone, other times we may not. However, the act of forgiving or seeking forgiveness is not based upon our feelings. It is based on our choice. We must choose to forgive or seek forgiveness because it is the right thing to do.

There have been times when I have reacted to Dottie in a less-than-loving manner. And sometimes I felt my cutting words were justified, sort of like she deserved what she got. At those moments it is difficult for me to realize or admit that I was wrong or feel like seeking her forgiveness. Yet in my heart and head I know Scripture says that love is not "rude. It does not demand its own way. It is not irritable..." (1 Corinthians 13:5).

What do you do in those situations? You know you shouldn't have said the things you said, yet you don't feel like seeking forgiveness. At that moment you may even feel that he or she is the one who needs to apologize.

What I've learned is that when my emotions contradict God's truth, I need to obey the truth whether I feel like it or not. And here is the amazing thing: My feelings will follow my feet. In other words, once I start taking steps to do the right thing, my feelings will follow.

There are times when I take myself by the collar, so to speak, and walk myself into the room and apologize to Dottie whether I feel like it or not. Sometimes I might start my apology somewhat like this, "I know I shouldn't have said what I said the way I said it. That was wrong of me." At this point I may not have much feeling behind my words but I continue. "Dottie, I know what I said hurt you, and I don't want to hurt you." About this time my voice is softening. I'm beginning to see past my harsh feelings and see the person I love—the person I have hurt. "You are the dearest person to me in all the world, and what I said was said in anger. I'm so sorry

I hurt the woman I love." By this time my feelings are catching up with what I'm saying. The choice to forgive or seek forgiveness may bring tears and appropriate emotions.

No, you may not feel like forgiving or seeking forgiveness at times, but choose to love by doing the right thing, and your feelings will follow. The choice to forgive calls you to take the initiative. When you move your feet, your feelings fall in line. Aren't you glad Jesus loves you so much that he took the initiative to die for you, even when you didn't deserve it? When you have experienced such mercy and grace, it empowers you to give mercy and grace to those who need forgiveness.

More Than Forgiving Others

Forgiving those you love is necessary if you are going to experience a deepened, intimate relationship. Seeking forgiveness is also necessary to maintain your connection to the one you love. Yet there is another aspect of forgiving, and that is *forgiving yourself*. At times that can be even more difficult than forgiving others.

The little restaurant was buzzing with activities. I was seated around the table having dinner with about seven other men from the community. They were all friends of mine. During the course of conversation I made an offhand insensitive remark that hurt Dave, one of my friends. I, however, was unaware that what I said had hurt him.

As I was driving home it began to dawn on me what I had said. I thought, *That may have really offended Dave.* I turned around and headed back to the restaurant in hope he was still there. I needed to apologize to him.

He was still at the restaurant. I pulled him aside and said, "Hey, Dave, I realized what I said was insensitive and wrong of me. I sensed I hurt you, and I'm sorry. Will you forgive me?"

To my amazement he said, "No!"

I thought I must have heard him wrong, so I tried again.

He said, "Well, you never should have said it!"

Of course, I wouldn't have returned to the restaurant if I hadn't realized I was wrong to have made the remark! So I tried once more to explain it to him, and he repeated, "You should have known better than to have said something like that. So no, you're not forgiven."

Now I'm sure there have been other people who haven't forgiven me for something, but they've never come right out and said it. Dave's words shocked me and actually shook me up emotionally. I began to beat myself up for being so stupid to say what I had. Essentially, I knew I had done wrong. I had even apologized to my friend for it. But now I was getting so down on myself that I joined Dave—I didn't forgive myself. I was miserable.

Self-condemnation—the refusal to let yourself off the hook—is epidemic in relationships today. When you and I condemn ourselves (refuse to forgive ourselves for what we have done or failed to do), we create a barrier in our love relationships. Remember that in an earlier chapter we talked about the critical need to love yourself in order to love your neighbor? If you can't love yourself enough to forgive yourself, you're going to have a very difficult time expressing love to your spouse or that special person in your life.

There is an antidote for self-condemnation. It's called gratefulness. After feeling sorry for myself for quite some time, it finally dawned on me: Jesus went to a cruel death so I could be forgiven of my sins. And if I couldn't forgive myself for what I did even though he had forgiven me, that reflected an ungrateful heart. I sure didn't want to be ungrateful, so I said, "Lord, I've asked you to forgive me of the foolish remark I made to Dave, and I know you have forgiven me. I was undeserving, but in your gracious mercy you have forgiven me. I want you to know how grateful I am for your forgiveness. To demonstrate it I will accept your forgiveness to the point of forgiving myself."

That was it. My gratitude for God's forgiveness empowered me to accept my own self-forgiveness. I was free. My misery turned into grateful joy. And my joy really irritated Dave. He thought I should stay miserable, but I didn't. In fact I went out of my way to express my love to him, and that irritated him even more. This went on for about a year. Eventually my freedom and kindness won him back as a dear friend. The relationship healed, and we became closer friends than we had been before. Being grateful for God's forgiveness can free us to forgive ourselves.

Some Reasons We Don't Forgive

There are no valid excuses for withholding forgiveness from someone who has offended you. There are, however, reasons we find it difficult to forgive.

Insecurity is one reason we don't forgive. If you or I feel insecure with ourselves or in our relationships, we might look for every opportunity to be assertive. Getting "one up" on someone by not forgiving them can provide a certain false sense of security.

Holding a grudge is another reason we don't forgive. There is a certain kind of pleasure in holding on to an attitude of resentment.

Many years ago I spoke at Cal Poly, Pomona, California, on the revolution of love. After my talk, a young woman came up to me. She said, "You know, Mr. McDowell, I really appreciated what you shared today, but I would not want the love for people that you have."

That really hit me! "Why not?" I asked.

"Because," she said, "I want the joy of hating those who hate me!"

Sometimes we don't forgive because we want to relish "the right to resent."

Self-pity can keep us from forgiving. That's the feeling that maintains, "Oh, I've been hurt more than anyone, and I just can't forgive anymore!"

Shifting the blame can block us from extending forgiveness. That's the feeling that "I was in the right, and I had a right to do what I did."

Plain old anger at a person can "justify" why we shouldn't forgive.

Judging a repeat offender is a classic excuse for not forgiving a person. How can you forgive someone who keeps repeating the same offense? Are you to forgive those who don't even ask for your forgiveness—let alone those who repeatedly offend you? Yes. Jesus went even further. He said to "love your enemies" (Matthew 5:44) and to keep forgiving regardless of how many times a person wrongs you. He said to forgive "seventy times seven" (Matthew 18:22), which is another way of saying your forgiveness of others is to be limitless.

When "Oh, I'm Sorry, Honey" Isn't Enough

Hypothetical: Dottie is late for an appointment. As she is rushing around and gathering things from the kitchen counter she bumps my coffee mug. I scramble back to keep from getting my leg scalded. "Oh, I'm so sorry, honey. I've got to run." Off she scurries out the door.

Was "Oh, I'm so sorry, honey" enough for that situation? Sure. No real damage was done, and anyway, accidents happen. I don't think Dottie needs to feel too upset over a spilled cup of coffee. It's really no big deal.

But some things in life *are* a big deal. And when they are, "Oh, I'm sorry, honey" isn't enough. When we cause real pain in the life of our loved one, more is needed than a simple apology. Our seeking forgiveness needs to include what the Bible calls *repentance*.

The apostle Paul said, "Godly sorrow brings repentance" (2 Corinthians 7:10). When our acts or attitudes of self-centeredness or self-reliance cause hurt in our spouse, we need to experience a godly sorrow that prompts us to repent of what we've done. We need to seek forgiveness. And here is an important principle about seeking forgiveness. The depth of healing in the relationship caused by painful hurts is proportionate to the depth of your understanding of the pain you caused. When you truly grasp just how much you have hurt your loved one, it highly motivates you to avoid hurting him or her in that way again.

My friends Dr. David and Teresa Ferguson introduced me to this principle. They provide a living example of how seeking forgiveness through repentance results in emotional healing and relational oneness. They tell their story in the excellent marriage book *Never Alone*.

David and Teresa were both 16 years old when they gave their parents an ultimatum: "Give us permission to marry or we'll elope to a state where we can get married legally without your permission." Neither of them were Christians at the time. David said their rebellious spirits brought pain to their parents and ultimately to themselves. Here the two of them tell their own story, which gives powerful insight into effective and ineffective ways to seek forgiveness.

> Teresa and I spent our wedding night in a local motel. Early the next morning while Teresa was still asleep, a friend of mine knocked on the door of our room. Stanley and I were pool-shooting buddies, and he wanted me to go shoot pool with him. The fact that I was on my honeymoon didn't seem to matter to Stanley, and it didn't make much difference to me. I loved shooting pool, so I got dressed, and we left for the pool hall. It never entered my mind to tell Teresa, who was still asleep when I walked out the door.

> Teresa tells what happened next: "When I woke up and found David and his car gone, I didn't know what to think. Had I displeased him already? Had he changed his mind about being married to me? I was only sixteen years old, and I felt confused and abandoned. So I left the motel and walked the several blocks home to my parents, crying and feeling very alone."

> When I (David) finally showed up at Teresa's parents' house and found her crying, I knew I had blown it. I said something like, "I shouldn't have done that. Now let's go." I displayed about as much depth of understanding for her

pain and sympathy as I would ordering a pizza. I kind of confessed my offense, and she kind of forgave me. And that's where the issue lay buried for the next fifteen years. My numbness to the magnitude of Teresa's pain contributed to a lack of intimacy from day one of our marriage.

After I became a Christian, I addressed the issue again. I think I said something like, "That was *really* wrong of me to go off to shoot pool that morning. Please forgive me." Still, I had not connected with the depth of her pain, so the issue was buried again for several more years.

I was coming to grips with my self-centeredness and a deeper understanding of how godly sorrow leads to repentance. I knew that Teresa's honeymoon pain was still an unresolved issue between us. And so, more than fifteen years after the event, I sat down with her, desiring to show respect and consideration for my wife and our need for deepened oneness.

Feeling a significant amount of anxiety, I said, "Teresa, I want you to tell me about the pain you felt that morning at the motel. Take as long as you need; I want to listen. I want to understand how deeply I hurt you that day."

When you approach your spouse like that, you are in effect taking off all your protective armor and dropping your guard. You are opening yourself up to truth and honesty that may be painful for you to hear. But exposing the depth of the pain you contributed is critical to the healing process, both for you and your spouse. First, the process of understanding your spouse's pain is for your benefit, to effect godly sorrow and a true repentance that will minimize repeat offenses. Second, as you mourn with your spouse over the magnitude of the pain, God can prompt in him or her both deepened forgiveness and freedom from fear.

Teresa talked for almost a half hour—which seemed to me like four hours. God's work in her heart allowed her to express her feelings with "I" messages instead of accusing "you" messages.

"When I woke up all alone," she said, "I felt so betrayed and afraid. I sensed such deep rejection that I began to question my importance to you or to anyone."

As she described in detail the betrayal, fear, uncertainty, and hurt she felt, my heart broke. I saw that confused sixteen-year-old girl walking home to her parents feeling used, abused, and abandoned.

Teresa and I wept that day over the suffering I had caused. With new understanding and a contrite heart, broken now to the depth of her pain, I said, "Teresa, I am so sad for the pain I caused you. It hurts me deeply that you hurt like that. Will you forgive me?"

Her reply was powerfully reassuring: "I did that years ago, but it means so much to me that you care about my hurt." Our marriage experienced a new measure of intimacy as a fifteen-year-old incident was bathed in tears of true repentance and the blessing of genuine comfort.[1]

Your marriage may not have experienced that much pain, but we all have contributed a measure of pain to the one we love. Take the initiative and invite your spouse to share with you the pain that you may have caused. Accept responsibility for what you have done by first doing your best to identify with the pain he or she has suffered. Secondly, resist the sort of guilt that can easily turn into resentment for your own distress. Embrace godly sorrow. Paul reminds us that "worldly sorrow, which lacks repentance, results in spiritual death" (2 Corinthians 7:10 NLT). Godly sorrow—true repentance—will reassure and comfort your spouse. You're acknowledging that you were the cause of his or her pain, and you're really sorry.

Seeking forgiveness from your spouse within the context of godly repentance leads to freedom, healing, and relational oneness. I have often prayed this prayer asking God to make me a more forgiving person. Join me in this prayer:

> *Heavenly Father, thank you for your mercy and grace that has forgiven me. I want to forgive as you do. Prompt me to take the initiative to seek forgiveness of those I offend. I want to understand the depth of pain I have caused another so that healing can take place. Help me to graciously forgive others that hurt me, even if they don't ask. Give me a sensitive, caring, and forgiving heart. Let me be a channel of your forgiveness to my spouse, my family, and to the world around me. In Jesus' name, amen.*

11

COMMITMENT #9

I Choose to Love You by
Making Money Matter

That is a great-looking rocking chair," I said as I ran my hand over the early American antique rocker. Liz, newly married to Alex, beamed as she commented on the unique wood grain patterns of the rocker. Alex made a grunting sound and then asked me to have a seat on the couch.

The couple had asked me to their home for some counsel. I had no idea that my admiration of the antique rocker had anything to do with their marital problems.

Turns out he wanted the house decorated in Mediterranean style furniture, and she wanted early American antique furniture. They had not discussed their home-decoration preferences before marriage, and now it had become a major source of contention. They wanted my counsel. Actually they wanted me to referee their fight.

She had a portion of the house she called "hers" that was decorated as she wanted. He had a section called "his" decorated in his preferred style. Their conversations were continually punctuated with "This is mine" and "That is yours."

On their first Christmas together Alex bought his new wife a beautiful gift—a Mediterranean desk stand. He probably could have purchased her a jackhammer and gotten a warmer response. Tragically, this marriage ended in divorce.

Yours, Mine, or Ours?

If you want your relationship to deepen into an intimate oneness, you need to choose to make money matter. In other words, relational unity isn't complete unless the two of you agree about material possessions and money matters.

Money problems within marital relationships are a major cause of conflict and divorce. Many couples work before marriage and have bank accounts, yet don't have meaningful conversations about how they are going to manage their money once they're married. Should they merge their accounts, keep individual accounts, or create a mix? Should the higher earner in the family get to spend more? Do they answer to each other for expenses? Is there a specific dollar amount that requires a discussion before one or the other makes a large purchase? How are decisions made about the style of home decorating, the model of car to purchase, the destination for a vacation, the budget, and so on?

Unless these and other issues are dealt with in an amicable way, you and your spouse can end up in a "yours" and "mine" quandary. If money matters are not approached properly, you can find yourself defending your possessions and your piece of the money pie—with your spouse defending his or hers. It would be wonderful if you could eliminate this struggle over what is "yours" and "mine" and agree that all money matters is a unified "ours." But if you are followers of Christ, do your possessions really belong to you 100 percent? Or does God own a percentage?

Many Christian couples believe that God requires a 10 percent minimum to be given to the church with the remaining 90 percent to be managed however they feel best. They get this from the Old Testament system of tithing: "One tenth of the produce of the land, whether grain from the fields or fruit from the trees, belongs to the Lord" (Leviticus 27:30).

The Levites (including the priests) received no tribal land. And the tithe was to support them. A second tithe was also to be given every third year for additional support of the Levites as well as of orphans, widows, and foreigners. This additional tenth was to be taken to the nearest town so that the needy might eat and be satisfied (see Deuteronomy 14:28; 26:12). Other offerings were also required of the children of Israel.

Some say this establishes a 10 percent contribution as a minimum for Christians today to pay to their local church. Others contend that this was a financial requirement for Israel and point out that it didn't amount to a minimum of 10 percent but rather a 13⅓ percent average annually (10 percent every year as a national tithe plus 10 percent every three years in addition as a local tithe). So what does God require of our money?

Jesus' teaching on this subject is very interesting. "You cannot become my disciple," Jesus said, "without giving up everything you own" (Luke 14:33). In the Chronicles it says "Everything in the heavens and on earth is yours, O LORD, and this is your kingdom" (1 Chronicles 29:11). Scripture indicates that God owns everything, and to be a Jesus follower we must relinquish our right to selfish ownership and become a faithful steward.

This makes a married couple (and all of us) stewards of what God allows us to "possess." It really isn't about what is yours, mine, or even ours—it's about what is *his*! When we see our earthly possessions in this light, it changes everything.

You Can't Keep What You Don't Give Away

Jesus said, "Give, and you will receive...The amount you give will determine the amount you get back" (Luke 6:38). That is quite different from what we normally think. From a human perspective, it's "take and you will get. The more you take the more you will get." But God's economic system works from a different premise.

The only things in life you can really keep are those you give away. Remember, love is other-focused. Giving is what love does; taking is what self-centeredness does. When you have a giving heart, you get love and protection and provision in return. A couple simply can't love and give to God while at the same time they are greedy and possessive of money. That is why Jesus said, "Use your worldly resources to benefit others and make friends. Then, when your earthly possessions are gone, they will welcome you to an eternal home...You cannot serve God and money" (Luke 16:9,13).

Dottie and I started from the very beginning agreeing on money matters. Many years ago in Austin, Texas, I asked her to marry me. To celebrate our engagement I planned to take her to a very nice (and expensive) restaurant. A few days earlier I had learned that a friend of mine needed a back brace due to an accident, but he didn't have the money for it. I shared my friend's predicament with Dottie. We both agreed we should take the engagement celebration money and buy a back brace. This left us with enough money to go to a fast-food restaurant to celebrate. That was the most meaningful engagement celebration we could have ever enjoyed. We had given—and then God gave us an incredible sense of mutual satisfaction and joy in knowing we were helping someone in need.

That night was a beginning of a lifetime of giving for us. Each year we have used a significant percentage of our income—beyond what we give to our church—to help others. Whether we provide scholarship funds for students, equipment for the handicapped, or food and clothing for orphans, we always seem to get back more than we give. But I have had to remind myself on more than one occasion that no matter how generous I feel, I need to be sure Dottie is in agreement. Our money belongs to God, yet both of us are co-stewards of that money.

God doesn't call you to stewardship so you will be poor; he wants you to be generous so you and others will experience his goodness. "Your generosity will result in thanksgiving to God...Others will praise God for the obedience that accompanies your confession of the gospel of Christ...And in their prayers for you their hearts will go out to you, because of the surpassing grace God has given you"

(2 Corinthians 9:11,13,14 NIV). When you give to him, he'll meet your need and enable you to continue giving. This is what good stewardship is all about—managing what he gives you, recognizing his ultimate ownership and his loving care for all his people. Live in the spirit of giving, and you will never go without. The apostle Paul makes that clear:

> You must each decide in your heart how much to give. And don't give reluctantly or in response to pressure. "For God loves a person who gives cheerfully." And God will generously provide all you need. Then you will always have everything you need and plenty left over to share with others. As the Scriptures say, "They share freely and give generously to the poor. Their good deeds will be remembered forever"...Yes, you will be enriched in every way so that you can always be generous (2 Corinthians 9:7-9,11).

What a difference it makes when a husband and wife accept God's principles of finance! The arguments about what's "mine" and what's "yours" melt away. The questions then revolve around "How will he be honored by the way we handle the money he has entrusted to us?"

God has a lot to say about finances. There are over 700 verses in the Bible dealing with money or possessions. Over two-thirds of the parables of Jesus speak about possessions or money matters. The important thing is to see ourselves as faithful stewards of what God has given us. He wants us to be faithful and responsible with what he has entrusted to us so we can hear him say, "Well done, my good and faithful servant" (Matthew 25:23).

Being a good steward means being a wise manager of money and other assets. That requires that you know how to use what you have for the right reasons.

There was a rich young man who came to Jesus inquiring, "What good things must I do to have eternal life?" (Matthew 19:16). On the surface Jesus' answer may seem strange because he eventually told the man to sell all he had, give the money to the poor, and "then come, follow me" (Matthew 19:21). Some conclude that Jesus is against having money. But that wasn't Jesus' point. He was trying to re-order the rich man's priorities. This man had put his trust in his wealth; Jesus wanted the young man to place his trust in him.

God wants you to use money, but he doesn't want you to put your trust in it. Take a look at a United States dollar bill. It doesn't say, "In This Money We Trust." You will notice it says, "In God We Trust." This is precisely what he wants. Read what Paul told Timothy:

> Teach those who are rich in this world not to be proud and not to trust in their money, which is so unreliable. Their trust should be in God, who richly gives us all we need for our enjoyment. Tell them to use that money to do good. They should be rich in good works and generous to those in need, always being ready to share with others (1 Timothy 6:17-18).

God wants you to learn to enjoy what he has given you as a couple and at the same time to be generous. Putting your trust in him, not your money, requires some very practical stewardship steps. It requires setting priorities and managing a budget as stewards directly accountable to him.

Priorities and Budget Management

The first order of business is to get on the same page with your spouse by agreeing that God owns all you possess and the two of you will trust in him to provide for your family. If you are not yet married but seriously dating someone, you should discuss this trusting in God and stewardship principle. Once you and the person you love agree that you both are to manage what he grants you, the entire discussion changes. As I have said, it is no longer about what is "mine" or "yours," but "how we honor God with what he has given us."

Next, there are two very important topics to tackle as you begin to manage the money God has given you: establish financial priorities and maintain a budget.

Establish financial priorities. What is more important to you: Going on one or two vacations a year or saving for a down payment on a home? Is a car payment on a *new* car more important than establishing a college fund for your child? Is going out to eat each week more important than giving to feed hungry children in Ethiopia? In other words, you need to establish your financial goals and prioritize them.

Remember I stated earlier that every misunderstanding usually develops as a result of differing assumptions. You and your spouse or loved one need to write out your financial assumptions. Talk them through. Put them on paper. Pray together about them. And then come to mutual agreement. This will enable you to know what percentage of income you will give to your church, set aside in a college fund, save for a vacation, put aside for retirement, and so on.

As you do this, a financial plan and a set of goals will emerge. Ask whether your goals are realistic and achievable. Set target dates and deadlines for your priorities and goals. Work together, and keep each other's strengths in play as you establish your financial priorities. One of you may be more prone to spend while the other more prone to save. One may say, "Let's get the cheaper item," while the other says, "Let's go for the quality item—it will last longer." These different perspectives can be a source of contention or can be a source of strength. Keep other-focused, and you can use your differing views as an advantage.

Manage a budget. To some a financial budget may seem like a restrictive burden that keeps them from spending what they want to spend. The truth is: A budget frees you up to spend what you need to spend. A budget in its simplest form is a projection of income and expenses. It is a written plan of action that should give you confidence that you are serving God wisely with your money.

It is not difficult to establish and manage a budget effectively. Take advantage of available software programs that provide a full range of household budgeting management. Some of the most common ones are Quicken for Home, Microsoft Money, and iCash; many more exist. These will guide you through the process of forming a budget and maintaining it week after week.

Begin by establishing your projected annual income. Start with your net income after taxes. Next project your expenses. This is where most people make mistakes—they don't accurately project their expenses.

To accurately create your budget you need to take four areas into account. If you don't it will be nearly impossible to live within your budget. And when you don't have enough money to pay your bills, tension can build within your relationship. Busting your budget is not good stewardship. Here are the four critical areas to follow to help you stay within budget:

Ongoing expenses based on past expenses. Normally you will have monthly expenses such as electric, gas, trash pickup, gasoline for the car, groceries, eating out (entertainment), and so on. You may also have a mortgage or car payment. To project expenses, look at what you paid out monthly over the course of the previous year.

You also must take into account those annual or semi-annual expenses such as property taxes, car insurance, health insurance, and life insurance. Divide these lump-sum expenses over a calendar year, then add your other monthly costs to determine your average expenses per month.

By including the monthly allotment for property taxes, car insurance, and so on, you will have saved money to pay those bills when they come due. This makes sense to many people, but the next budget area is what most people overlook.

Save for major replacement and repair. Let's say Alison and Joey have established their monthly budget and have enough to cover their expenses, including a clothing allowance for Alison and a vacation budget to cover a Caribbean cruise this winter. Everything is going just fine until the furnace goes out. To replace it will cost $6500!

Joey and Alison have only $1500 in savings. What do they do? Joey says they can pay the bill if they take from the vacation budget and cut out Alison's clothing allowance for six months. Alison says, "No way!" and claims that an emergency like this is what the credit card is for. Tensions rise, and a battle over the budget ensues.

What Joey and Alison have overlooked are the long-term expenses of owning their own home. Every day your appliances, heating and cooling equipment, bathroom fixtures, furniture, flooring, roof, siding, and so on are slowly wearing out. If you don't budget a monthly amount and set it aside for these kinds of future expenses, you will be unprepared to cover them when the time comes.

Another major replacement item many overlook is a car. Even if you buy a car outright and owe nothing on it, your car is steadily depreciating. In five, six, or eight years, what is it going to be worth? Unless you budget and save an adequate amount each month, you will not be prepared with a lump sum to purchase another car—unless you go in debt. Unfortunately most families are debt-heavy, and the cost of interest drags them down financially and emotionally.

To avoid being caught with "unexpected" expenses, expect them. Calculate the average lifespan of your appliances, heating and cooling equipment, roofing, furniture, flooring, and so on. Determine when you want to redecorate and when you will want to replace the car. Then divide the years for using each item into its projected replacement cost. This will give you the annual and then monthly amount you will need to hold back in order to be prepared when those items need to be replaced, redecorated, or repaired.

Evaluate and adjust. The only way to be accurate and effectively manage your budget is to continually evaluate where you are financially and make adjustments when necessary. Avoiding financial pressure requires hard choices. When you see you are about to go over budget, you either need to cut somewhere, bring in more income, or both. Living within budget isn't always easy, but it is nearly impossible to accomplish unless you continually evaluate your financial situation and make the necessary adjustments.

Create and maintain a buffer. Even after you put money aside for major replacement and repairs, there will be the truly unexpected expenses you will need money to cover. Financial advisors call this provision the "emergency fund." It can cover things like the need to travel across the country to the funeral when an unexpected death in the family occurs. You may have an accident or an illness that keeps you off work for an extended period of time and isn't covered by a disability policy. You may not be able to save enough for every conceivable eventuality, but you need some form of emergency fund. Experts say this fund should equal 25 percent of your annual income. The point is to be prepared as much as possible for the truly unexpected.

Plan Together and Keep Focused

When it comes to money matters you continually need to choose to listen to each other, communicate effectively, be other-focused, resolve conflicts quickly, and be forgiving. It's not always easy to get on the same page. The key is to plan your financial present and future together and then stay focused on that plan. You will find that as you discuss your dreams, concerns, needs, and hopes, you will open up a new channel for communication in your marriage and draw closer in the give-and-take of financial planning. More importantly, your stewardship will then bring honor to God.

About your planning. If you have already established your financial priorities and a working budget, most of your decisions about money matters have already been made. Your financial boundaries have been established. If you have yet to set priorities and budget, work through your financial plan when you are free of an immediate money crunch. You want your discussions of budget and financial boundaries to be as free of financial pressures as possible. Be as objective as possible when discussing your financial priorities.

Once your budget is in place, you are ready to make purchase or expenditure decisions. All you need to do is consult your budget. If it's not in the budget, you most likely forgo the purchase. If on the other hand, the item in question is something you really need to make a priority, then you sit down together to "evaluate and adjust." You may not need to meet weekly with your spouse on financial issues, but you do need a systematic time to evaluate and adjust your plan. The key is to do it together.

About debt. The simple rule is, "Don't live beyond your means." Credit, like money itself, is neither good nor bad. It all depends on how you use it. However, when not handled properly, credit can become a tremendous burden.

According to CreditCards.com "the average American household with at least one credit card carries nearly $15,950 in credit card debt."[1] The average interest rate on that debt runs in the mid-to-high teens. Since many households also have a home mortgage and car payment, it means we are burdened with debt.

There is no quicker way to experience financial bondage than by the improper use of credit. Solomon said, "Just as the rich rule the poor, so the borrower is servant to the lender" (Proverbs 22:7). Avoid debt as much as possible. Manage your budget, live within your means, save, and plan toward being debt-free—a freedom that can bring great joy to a marriage relationship.

About record-keeping. Another priority—and part of your planning—should include organizing your financial records. You can begin by going over the following list with your spouse. The idea is for both of you to know where everything is located and passwords where applicable.

Document/item	Location/how to access
Budget	
Bank accounts	
Birth certificates	
Auto title(s)	
House deed/rental contract	
Investment list: Stocks, bonds, mutual funds, retirement accounts, savings accounts	

Beneficiary forms	
Last will and testament	
Power of attorney: financial	
Power of attorney: health care; or living will (advanced medical directive)	
Insurance policies: Auto Homeowner's Life Health Long-term health	
Current tax information	
Past tax returns	

List of contacts: lawyers, investment advisers, insurance agents, and so on	
Safe-deposit box and key	
Guide to digital assets (including passwords)	
Funeral arrangements	

While one of you may be the primary person who does most of the financial management in your relationship/family, both of you need to know where all the records are located. It is best that both spouses are able to manage the finances of the home. I have seen the pressure that develops when one spouse passes away and the other doesn't have a clue how to manage the finances. Avoid that pressure by teaching one another how to carry out the tasks you both perform, so that either of you can take on the other's role if necessary. In all likelihood the day will come when one of you will need to temporarily or permanently fill the other's role.

If you don't have a will, health-care power of attorney, or financial power of attorney, meet with an attorney to get it done. The sooner you can work on your estate planning the better. Newly married couples should have a will and these important documents drawn up within their first year of marriage. "Good planning and hard work lead to prosperity, but hasty shortcuts lead to poverty" (Proverbs 21:5).

Take advantage of financial-planning books and seminar courses like those offered by Dave Ramsey, for example, "Financial Peace University," "The Total Money Makeover," "Relating with Money," and so on.

Choose to love your spouse by making money matter. This will lead to becoming good and faithful stewards of God's provision. As you do you will honor him, with the added bonus of meeting your spouse's need for security. Happy couples are couples who manage their finances together.

12

COMMITMENT #10

I Choose to Love You by
Keeping My Love Life Fresh and Alive

Its shores are barren. The atmosphere is harsh. Its bitter waters can not sustain life nor can it quench your thirst. It is called the Dead Sea.

In contrast, another body of water is a scene of beauty, a center of commerce whose shores teem with life. Carpeted slopes of rich grass encircle this sea. It is called the Sea of Galilee.

What makes the difference between a dead sea and a sea full of life? One receives fresh water daily from the Jordan River but holds onto it. The water becomes still and stagnant. That's the Dead Sea. The other receives water too but keeps the water moving by giving it away. It takes in water from the northern mountains and allows that water to flow through it to the winding Jordan River at its south. That's the Sea of Galilee.

One stands still, letting things be as they are—and it dies. The other is on the move, both receiving and giving out—and it stays fresh and alive. A marriage is similar. You can simply receive, taking in all the love you can get and enjoying the relationship—yet that satisfaction to let things be as they are can make your relationship stagnant. Do this and it may die. Or, you can both receive and also give love in return, looking for ways to renew your marriage. Do that and your relationship will remain fresh, alive, and vibrant.

King Solomon talked about people who give and keep the relationship fresh:

> It is possible to give freely and become more wealthy, but those who are stingy will lose everything. The generous prosper and are satisfied; those who refresh others will themselves be refreshed (Proverbs 11:24-25 NLT).

I told you about Mark in a previous chapter. He was the husband who said his marriage with his wife, Susan, had grown lifeless and stale. He thought he had explored all he could of her, and she became dull to him. His relationship was dying. But Mark woke up and grabbed hold of the principles that keep relationships alive and well. Couples who keep their marriage relationship fresh have implemented the principles of an active, moving, and growing relationship. I will share here five principles that have been instrumental in keeping my relationship with Dottie fresh and alive for over 40 years.

Continually Cultivate the Relationship

Like aerobic conditioning, a love relationship is not static. It is either growing or atrophying. And for a relationship to stay alive, grow, and mature it must be continually cultivated.

When I first got married I was convinced my relationship with Dottie would grow and last. I believed a relationship could be kept vibrant, but I hadn't yet experienced the day-in, day-out of married life. I remember, just after I was married, speaking to about 300 faculty members and administrators at the University of Tennessee. As I usually did during the first few minutes of a talk, I made some comments about my wife—how excited I was to be married and how I looked forward to a lifetime of happiness with Dottie.

Suddenly a young professor in his late twenties interrupted my talk and asked in a sarcastic tone, "How long have you been married?"

"Six months," I replied. He then made a sad statement I've heard many times. "Just wait and see how you talk after you've been married for five years!"

Before becoming engaged I had already been speaking on the secret of loving, and people would echo that same sentiment, "Let's see how you talk when you're engaged!" After I was engaged, their comments changed. They said to just wait until I was married. After I was married, they said that I'd change my tune after five years, and then after ten, and then after twenty.

I was sure these people were wrong. My philosophy, however, has always been that a man with experience has an advantage over a man with an argument. So, standing in front of this prestigious audience at the University of Tennessee, it seemed that the professor had the advantage of experience. It was one of the few times in my life when I was at a loss for words.

Just then a man in the back stood up and walked up to the front. He was about 75 years old. I didn't know who he was. I learned later he was Roger Rusk, a dynamic Christian, a highly respected professor at the university, and brother of former Secretary of State Dean Rusk.

He walked to the front row and looked me square in the eye. Then he turned toward the vocal professor, leaned over, and said, "Mister, it gets *better* after fifty-five years!" I was relieved that someone with experience validated my stated belief. Today I *know* a marriage relationship can grow and last. My relationship with Dottie is stronger, deeper, and more intimate now than I ever dreamed it could be, but this did not happen without continual cultivation. And how did we cultivate our relationship during these 40-plus years? By choosing—day-in, day-out—to make these ten commitments a way of life. Living out these commitments works. My deepened relationship over four decades with Dottie is living proof. We haven't implemented these commitments perfectly, but we keep at it. Cultivate your relationship in these ten ways, and your love life will also grow, expand, and remain fresh. The key is to keep at it. Let's review these ten commitments.

1. Cultivate your relationship by *loving God with everything you've got.* He will empower you to love your closest neighbor—your spouse—with an unselfish, other-focused love. That will help keep your love life fresh and alive.

2. Cultivate your relationship by *loving and accepting yourself for who you are*—a person created by God and accepted by him. Loving yourself unselfishly is a prerequisite to truly loving your spouse, and that will help keep your love life fresh and alive.

3. Cultivate your relationship by *making the security, happiness, and welfare of your spouse as important as your own* and by meeting the relational needs of the one you love. That will help keep your love life fresh and alive.

4. Cultivate your relationship by *being slow to speak and quick to listen to the words and heart of your lover.* That will help keep your love life fresh and alive.

5. Cultivate your relationship by *learning the art of communication* with the focus on how you can better connect with the heart and soul of the one you love. That will help keep your love life fresh and alive.

6. Cultivate your relationship by *demonstrating to your spouse that you accept him or her unconditionally, that your love is loyal, and that you will always, always be there*

for him or her. That will help keep your love life fresh and alive.

7. Cultivate your relationship by *resolving all conflicts quickly.* That will help keep your love life fresh and alive.

8. Cultivate your relationship by *always forgiving your spouse and seeking forgiveness* after you have sought to understand the depth of pain your offense has caused. That will help keep your love life fresh and alive.

9. Cultivate your relationship by *partnering with your spouse to become faithful stewards of the possessions God has given you.* That will help keep your love life fresh and alive.

10. Cultivate your relationship by *recognizing when you have become comfortable receiving the loving support of your spouse but forget to love back.* That will keep your love life fresh and alive.

Strive to cultivate your relationship in these ten ways until they become a way of life. Is that easy? No, but nothing of great worth in life comes without effort. Invest in your relationship in these areas, and you will reap a lifetime of happiness, meaning, and fulfillment.

There are a few other things that I have found that help keep the marriage relationship fresh and alive.

Let Go of the Unresolved

In chapter 9 I talked about the need to resolve conflicts quickly, and I stated that it is far more rewarding to resolve a conflict than to dissolve the relationship. That is all true, of course. Conflict resolution is critical to deepening a love relationship. Yet not all conflicts end in perfect resolution.

Remember, we are imperfect beings with emotional baggage.

We carry dysfunctions that at times seem to keep us from understanding how to resolve certain conflicts. When we encounter one of those unresolved issues, we must let it go.

There are a few conflicts in my relationship with Dottie that for years have surfaced and continue to surface but still go on unresolved. They are not major things, but to fully resolve them would probably take years and thousands of dollars in professional counseling. Is it necessary to dig down deep to get to the bottom of these issues so they don't disrupt the relationship? For major issues, absolutely yes—but for those minor areas that seem hard to resolve—let them go. That is what love does. "Show deep love for each other," the Bible says, "for love covers a multitude of sins" (1 Peter 4:8).

This doesn't mean you bury the unresolved differences; it means you forgive and let them go. Your spouse may never be able to understand how his or her dysfunction bothers you and may not even apologize for it. Let those minor unresolved issues go. Don't harbor them or bury them alive, but love and accept your spouse with all the imperfections and limitations he or she has and choose to give a "pass" on those issues. As I write this book I am hard-pressed to even remember those few differences that emerge between Dottie and me from time to time. That is because I have let them go and so don't hold them in mind. That is yet another way to keep your relationship fresh and alive.

Be Grateful

The three words "I love you" say a lot. But the more your spouse understands what that truly means by seeing the evidence of it in your daily behavior, the greater intimacy you will experience. In a large part that is what this book is about—putting meat and bones on experiencing real love. One of the dimensions of continuing to connect on a deeper level relationally is to express appreciation, praise, and thankfulness to the one you love. In other words, let your love come from a heart of gratefulness.

One of the things I tried to instill in my children was the importance of gratefulness. I often told them that one of the greatest sins was the sin of ingratitude. Learning to be grateful is a key principle for a fulfilling life and in keeping a relationship fresh and alive.

Fostering a grateful heart toward your spouse will pay huge dividends in very specific areas of your life. Scientists have conducted research aimed at understanding the positive effects of being grateful. Recently the University of California, Berkeley, began collaborating with the University of California, Davis, in a $5.6 million, three-year project called "Expanding the Science and Practice of Gratitude."[1] The idea was to promote practices of gratitude in medical, educational, and organizational settings to reap the benefits of being grateful.

Dr. Robert Emmons, a leading scientific expert on gratitude, contends that hundreds of studies have documented the social, physical, and psychological benefits of gratitude. He points out that practicing gratitude

- increases happiness and life satisfaction
- reduces anxiety and depression
- strengthens the immune system, lowers blood pressure, reduces symptoms of illness, and makes us less bothered by aches and pains
- helps us sleep better
- makes us more resilient, helping us recover more effectively from traumatic events
- strengthens relationships, making us feel closer and more connected to friends, family and spouse[2]

These studies conclude that when we become grateful, we develop better ways of coping with difficulties and handling stress in life. For example, grateful people tend to handle failure and negative circumstances with less stress and embrace success with more grace. Dr. Melanie Greenberg, clinical and health psychologist, says that practicing gratitude "opens the heart and activates positive emotion centers in the brain. Regular practice of gratitude can change the way our brain neurons fire into more positive automatic patterns."[3]

Is it any wonder God's Word tells us to "be thankful in all circumstances, for this is God's will for you who belong to Christ" (1 Thessalonians 5:18)? He wants us to live a life of joy. Being grateful is foundational to experiencing true joy in a relationship. "Give thanks to the LORD, for he is good!" wrote the psalmist. "His faithful love endures forever" (Psalm 136:11).

Make it a practice to thank your spouse for who he or she is— for his or her qualities and character, and for becoming the loving person he or she now is. You are actually saying, "I love you" when you say things like "You mean the world to me," "I am so thankful for you," "You make my life worth living," "I am so grateful you entered my life," "You complete me," and so on. Express a heart of gratitude to the one you love, and do it often. It will help keep your love life fresh and alive.

Enjoy Humor

"A cheerful heart is good medicine" (Proverbs 17:22). Humor is good for your health and good for your relationship.

Research shows that laughter boosts the immune system, lowers stress hormones, relaxes your muscles, and even helps to prevent heart disease.[4] The emotional and relational benefits of laughter have been shown to reduce depression, anxiety, and tension, increase hope and optimism, strengthen relationships, help defuse conflict, and promote group bonding.[5] There is a reason God gave you the gift of laughter. Use it to keep your relationship with your spouse fresh and alive.

At times I can feel the tension begin to rise. Dottie and I are about to have one of those conversations. Then it happens. One of us says something off the wall and ridiculous and the other one laughs. The tension is broken, and we often even forget what we were getting tense about. Humor defuses it all, and we realize just how much we enjoy each other.

Embrace humor as a constant companion in your relationship. Get to the place where you can laugh even at yourself. Often we treat some issues far more seriously than they deserve. Learn to joke with each other in a healthy way. Don't laugh *at* your spouse or make fun of him or her. Instead, laugh *with* your spouse and have fun together. The better you master the art of humor, the more it will help you keep your love life fresh and alive.

Be Spontaneous

You have probably heard it said that "variety is the spice of life." Well, spontaneity is its engine. Another thing that keeps a relationship fresh and vibrant is being romantically creative, spontaneously loving "out of the box," and surprising your spouse with "random" expressions of love.

Life can get routine, and your relationship can become common, comfortable, even a bit boring if you don't inject spontaneity into it. Your love relationship is an adventure—treat it like one.

It doesn't take an ingenious, creative mind to do things a little out of the ordinary. You were probably a little crazy and unpredictable when you were dating. Bring some of that craziness back once in a while.

Back in the '70s, a 36-year-old Miami housewife, Marabel Morgan, wrote a book—*The Total Woman*. Her marriage had been less than spectacular, and as a Christian she had sought out biblically based solutions. Her candor and spontaneity in fanning the flame of love shocked some. But she offered some unique ideas about being romantically creative. Here is one of them:

> One morning, Charlie remarked about the pressures of the day that lay ahead of him. All day I remembered his grim face as he drove away. Knowing he would feel weary and defeated, I wondered how I could revive him when he came home.
>
> For an experiment I put on pink baby-doll pajamas and white boots after my bubble bath. I must admit that I looked foolish and felt even more so. When I opened the door that night to greet Charlie, I was unprepared for his reaction. My quiet, reserved, nonexcitable husband took one look, dropped his briefcase on the doorstep, and chased me around the dining-room table. We were in stitches by the time he caught me, and breathless with that old feeling of romance.[6]

That kind of spontaneity may be a little much for you, but you get the idea. Try new things. Awaken that excited lover deep within you. It's still in there—sometimes it just needs to be jarred loose. Try dancing in the rain. Roll around together in the grass. Go parking (I mean actually make out in your car). There is no scriptural mandate to enjoy sexual relationships only in a bedroom. Be discreet in your sex life, but be creative.

Astonish your wife with two flowers that match the color of her eyes; surprise your husband with breakfast in bed—anything that sparks that adventurous and romantic aspect of your life. Part of being spontaneous is doing things out of the ordinary, exploring new places, and shaking things up to ignite the passion of love in you and your lover. Being spontaneous can help you keep your love life fresh and alive.

Marriage is a journey, an adventure to lovingly connect with another person for a lifetime. You were created to love and be loved. Choose to love the one God has given you, and make your love choices a conscious decision every day. As you do, you will find you are becoming an irresistible lover that has discovered the true secrets of loving.

Relational Needs
Assessment Inventory

Instructions

For each of the 50 statements below, enter the number that best represents your response to that statement. Then you may interpret your responses by completing the section "Identifying Your Top Needs." Ask your wife to take this inventory as well. If you have teenagers they can probably relate to most of the assessment test. Ask them to take it as well. You will probably need to score younger children by assessing how they would respond to each statement.

Strongly Disagree	Disagree	Neutral	Agree	Strongly Agree
-2	-1	0	+1	+2

____ **1.** It is important that people accept me for who I am, even if I'm a little "different."

____ **2.** It is very important to me that my financial world be in order.

____ **3.** I sometimes grow weary of doing my usual best.

____ **4.** It is important to me that others seek my opinion.

____ **5.** It is important that I receive frequent physical hugs, warm embraces, and so on.

____ **6.** I feel good when someone enters into my world and wants to know what I'm all about.

____ **7.** It is important for me to know where I stand with those who are in authority over me.

____ **8.** It is meaningful to me when someone notices that I need help and offers to get involved.

____ **9.** I often feel overwhelmed. When this happens, I need someone to come alongside me and lighten my load.

____ **10.** I feel blessed when someone notices and shows concern for how I'm doing emotionally.

____ **11.** I like to know if what I do is of value to others.

____ **12.** Generally speaking, I don't like a lot of solitude.

____ **13.** It means a lot to me when loved ones initiate an "I love you."

____ **14.** I resist being seen only as a part of a large group. Being recognized as an individual is important to me.

____ **15.** I feel blessed when someone calls just to hear me out and encourages me.

____ **16.** It is important to me that people acknowledge not only what I do but who I am.

____ **17.** I feel best when my world is orderly and somewhat predictable.

____ **18.** I am pleased when people acknowledge my work on a project and express gratitude.

____ **19.** I especially enjoy completing a task when I am surrounded by others who like being with me.

____ **20.** I feel good when others notice my strengths and gifts.

____ **21.** I sometimes feel overwhelmed and discouraged.

____ **22.** I want to be treated with kindness and equality by all, regardless of my race, gender, looks, and status.

____ **23.** Physical affection in marriage is very important to me.

____ **24.** I love it when someone wants to spend time with me alone.

____ **25.** I feel blessed when someone notices what I do and says, "Good job!"

____ **26.** It is meaningful to me to be held and cared for after a hard day.

____ **27.** Even when I am confident about my talents, gifts, and so on, I welcome input and help from others.

____ **28.** When I feel stressed out or down, sympathy and encouragement from other people are very meaningful to me.

____ **29.** I feel good when someone expresses satisfaction with the way I am.

____ **30.** I enjoy being in a group of people when they are talking positively about me.

____ **31.** I would describe myself as a touchy-feely person.

____ **32.** It is important that my input is considered in a decision that will affect my life or schedule.

___ **33.** I feel blessed when someone shows interest in the projects I am working on.

___ **34.** I like trophies, plaques, and special gifts which commemorate something significant I have done.

___ **35.** I sometimes worry about the future.

___ **36.** When in a new environment, I immediately search for a group of people to connect with.

___ **37.** The thought of moving, starting a new job or class, or making other changes fills me with anxiety.

___ **38.** It bothers me when people are prejudiced against others because they dress or act differently.

___ **39.** I need to be surrounded by friends and loved ones who will be there through thick and thin.

___ **40.** I feel blessed when someone thanks me for something I have done.

___ **41.** It is very meaningful to me to know that someone is praying for me.

___ **42.** I am bothered by people who try to control others.

___ **43.** I feel blessed when I receive undeserved and spontaneous expressions of love.

___ **44.** I am pleased when someone looks me in the eyes and really listens when I talk.

____ **45.** I feel blessed when people commend me for any godly characteristic I exhibit.

____ **46.** It is important to me to have a soul mate stand with me when I am hurting or in trouble.

____ **47.** I don't enjoy working alone. I would rather have someone working with me.

____ **48.** It is important to me to feel like I am a part of the group.

____ **49.** I respond positively when someone seeks to understand my emotions and shows me loving concern.

____ **50.** When working on a project, I would much rather work with a team of people than by myself.

Identifying Your Top Needs

INSTRUCTIONS:

Using the numbers (**-2, -1, 0, +1, +2**) that you placed in the blank in front of each item in the **Relational Needs Assessment Inventory**, add up the numbers to discover what your total is for each of the ten relational needs. Choose which of the ten needs represent your top three and the top three of your spouse. Discuss your findings with each other.

ACCEPTANCE

1. Add up your responses (-2, -1, 0, +1, +2) to statements:

1 _____
19 _____
36 _____
38 _____
48 _____
Total _____

These responses relate to the need for *acceptance.*

SECURITY

2. Add up your responses to statements:

2 _____
17 _____
35 _____
37 _____
39 _____
Total _____

These responses relate to the need for *security.*

APPRECIATION

3. Add up your responses to statements:

16 _____
18 _____
20 _____
34 _____
40 _____
Total _____

These responses relate to the need for *appreciation.*

ENCOURAGEMENT

4. Add up your responses to statements:

3 _____
15 _____
21 _____
33 _____
41 _____
Total _____

These responses relate to the need for *encouragement.*

RESPECT

5. Add up your responses
   to statements:

4	_____
14	_____
22	_____
32	_____
42	_____
Total	_____

   These responses relate to the
   need for *respect.*

AFFECTION

6. Add up your responses
   to statements:

5	_____
13	_____
23	_____
31	_____
43	_____
Total	_____

   These responses relate to the
   need for *affection.*

ATTENTION

7. Add up your responses
   to statements:

6	_____
12	_____
24	_____
30	_____
44	_____
Total	_____

   These responses relate to the
   need for *attention.*

APPROVAL

8. Add up your responses
   to statements:

7	_____
11	_____
25	_____
29	_____
45	_____
Total	_____

   These responses relate to the
   need for *approval.*

COMFORT

9. Add up your responses
to statements:

     10 _____
     26 _____
     28 _____
     46 _____
     49 _____
Total _____

These responses relate to the
need for *comfort.*

SUPPORT

10. Add up your responses
to statements:

     8 _____
     9 _____
     27 _____
     47 _____
     50 _____
Total _____

These responses relate to the
need for *support.*

Notes

Chapter 1—What Do You Want in a Relationship?

1. Tomas Chamorro-Premuzic, "Five Reasons Why Relationships Fail," *Psychology Today*, April 5, 2012.

Chapter 6—I Choose to Love You by Becoming a Great Listener

1. David Augsburger, *Caring Enough to Hear and Be Heard* (Ventura, CA: Regal Books, 1982), 104.

2. Augsburger, 149-150.

Chapter 9—I Choose to Love You by Resolving Conflicts Quickly

1. As quoted in *AARP Bulletin*, "Real Possibilities—The Poll, Love and Marriage," June 2013, 4.

Chapter 10—I Choose to Love You by Always Forgiving You

1. Adapted from David and Teresa Ferguson, *Never Alone* (Austin, TX: Intimacy Press, 2001) 31-32, 152, 155-156. Used by permission.

Chapter 11—I Choose to Love You by Making Money Matter

1. As quoted in *CNN Money*, "Money 101, Lesson 9: 'Controlling Your Personal Debt,'" http://money.cnn.com/magazines/moneymag/money101/lesson9/index.htm.

Chapter 12—I Choose to Love You by Keeping My Love Life Fresh and Alive

1. Steven E.F. Brown, "Thanksgiving: The Power of Gratitude," *San Francisco Business Times*, November 13, 2012.

2. Robert Emmons, "Why Gratitude is Good," as quoted in "Why Practice Gratitude?" *Greater Good: The Science of a Meaningful Life*, e-newsletter of the Greater Good Science Center, University of California, Berkeley, http://greatergood.berkeley.edu/topic/gratitude/definition#how_to_cultivate.

3. As quoted in Melanie Greenberg, "The Mindful Self-Express," *Psychology Today*, November 23, 2011.

4. K.H. Taber, M. Redden, R.A. Hurley, "Functional anatomy of humor: Positive affect and chronic mental illness," *Journal of Neuropsychiatry and Clinical Neurosciences* 2007, 359-362, as quoted in Dwenda Gjerdingen, "The Health Benefits of Humor and Laughter," The Network 2013, http://ag.org/wim/0805/0805_Laughter.cfm.

5. Taber et al.

6. Marabel Morgan, *The Total Woman* (Old Tappan, NJ: Fleming H. Revell Co., 1973), 94.

About the Author
and the Josh McDowell Ministry

As a young man, **Josh McDowell** was a skeptic of Christianity. However, while at Kellogg College in Michigan, he was challenged by a group of Christian students to intellectually examine the claims of Jesus Christ. Josh accepted the challenge and came face-to-face with the reality that Jesus was in fact the Son of God, who loved him enough to die for him. Josh committed his life to Christ, and for 50 years he has shared with the world both his testimony and the evidence that God is real and relevant to our everyday lives.

Josh received a bachelor's degree from Wheaton College and a master's degree in theology from Talbot Theological Seminary in California. He has been on staff with Cru (formerly Campus Crusade for Christ) for almost 50 years. Josh and his wife, Dottie, have been married for more than 40 years and have four grown children and ten grandchildren. They live in Southern California.

Other Resources from
Josh McDowell and Sean McDowell

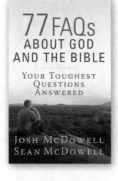

77 **FAQs About God and the Bible**

Most of us have honest questions about God and the Bible, but it's sometimes hard to know how to ask them—and who to ask. So Josh and Sean McDowell have identified the most frequently asked questions, and through extensive research and insight they provide answers to issues such as…

- What kinds of proofs are there that God exists?
- Where did evil come from?
- Isn't the Bible full of errors and contradictions?

And they tackle tough questions raised by today's skeptics, including…

- Why does God allow suffering?
- If God is so loving, why can't he be more tolerant of sin?
- Isn't it arrogant to claim Christianity is the only true religion?

Concise and accessible, *77 FAQs* gives you solid answers to help you better know why you believe and grow deeper in your faith.

Understanding Intelligent Design

Everything You Need to Know in Plain Language
William A. Dembski and Sean McDowell

> "*Understanding Intelligent Design*
> is the best book of its type."

J.P. Moreland
Author and Distinguished Professor
of Philosophy, Biola University

The prevailing mindset in our schools and in the media is that everything we see came into being strictly by accident. But in this user-friendly resource, William Dembski and Sean McDowell show that many scientists are now admitting that this viewpoint is not based on facts.

Understanding Intelligent Design clearly shows what the best information is revealing—that our existence is not an accidental by-product of nature but the clear result of intelligent design.

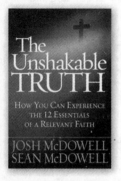

The Unshakable Truth®

How You Can Experience the 12 Essentials of a Relevant Faith

As a Christian, you may feel unsure about what you believe and why. Maybe you wonder if your faith is even meaningful and credible.

Unpacking 12 biblical truths that define the core of Christian belief and Christianity's reason for existence, this comprehensive yet easy-to-understand handbook helps you discover

- the foundational truths about God, his Word, sin, Christ, the Trinity, the church, and six more that form the bedrock of Christian faith

- how you can live out these truths in relationship with God and others

- ways to pass each truth on to your family and the world around you

Biblically grounded, spiritually challenging, and full of practical examples and real-life stories, *The Unshakable Truth* is a resource applicable to every aspect of everyday life.

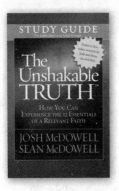

The Unshakable Truth® Study Guide

This study guide offers you—or you and your group—a *relational experience* to discover...

- 12 foundational truths of Christianity—in sessions about God, his Word, the Trinity, Christ's atonement, his resurrection, his return, the church, and five more
- "Truth Encounter" exercises to actually help you live out these key truths
- "TruthTalk" assignments on ways to share the essentials of the faith with your family and others

Through twelve 15-minute Web-link videos, Josh and Sean McDowell draw on their own father-son legacy of faith to help you feel adequate to impart what you believe with confidence. *Includes instructions for group leaders.*

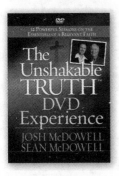

The Unshakable Truth™ DVD Experience

12 Powerful Sessions on the Essentials of a Relevant Faith

What do I believe, and why do I believe it? How is it relevant to my life? How do I live it out?

If you're asking yourself questions like these, you're not alone. In 12 quick, easy-to-grasp video sessions based on their book *The Unshakable Truth*, Josh and Sean McDowell give a solid introduction to the foundations of the faith.

Josh and Sean outline 12 key truths with clear explanations, compelling discussions, and provocative "on-the-street" interviews. And uniquely, they explain these truths *relationally*, showing you how living them out changes you and affects family and friends—everyone you encounter. *Helpful leader's directions included.*

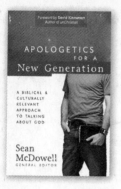

Apologetics for a New Generation
A Biblical and Culturally Relevant Approach to Talking About God
Sean McDowell, general editor

This generation's faith is constantly under attack from the secular media, skeptical teachers, and unbelieving peers. You may wonder, *How can I help?*

Working with young adults every day, Sean McDowell understands their situation and shares your concern. His first-rate team of contributors shows how you can help members of the new generation plant their feet firmly on the truth. Find out how you can walk them through the process of...

- formulating a biblical worldview and applying scriptural principles to everyday issues
- articulating their questions and addressing their doubts in a safe environment
- becoming confident in their faith and effective in their witness

The truth never gets old, but people need to hear it in fresh, new ways. Find out how you can effectively share the answers to life's big questions with a new generation.